BACKCOUNTRY FURY

A Sixteen-Year-Old Patriot in the Revolutionary War

By Dr. Tony Zeiss

Wake Forest, NC
www.scuppernongpress.com

Backcountry Fury
A Sixteen-Year-Old Patriot in the Revolutionary War
Dr. Tony Zeiss

Copyright © 2010, 2024 Dr. Tony Zeiss

The Scuppernong Press
PO Box 1724
Wake Forest, NC 27588
www.scuppernongpress.com

Second Printing

All rights reserved. No part of this book may be reproduced or transmitted in any form or by any means. Electronic, or mechanical, including photocopying, recording or by any information storage and retrieval system, without permission in writing from the publisher. No abridgment or changes to the text are authorized by the publisher.

Book cover art by Dan Nance, Patriot Art, Inc.

Library of Congress Cataloging-in-Publication Data
Zeiss, Anthony.
Backcountry fury: a sixteen-year-old patriot in the Revolutionary War / by Tony Zeiss. cm.
ISBN 978-1-942806-67-7
Young, Thomas, 1764-1848—Juvenile literature. 2. South Carolina—History— Revolution, 1775-1783—Biography—Juvenile literature. 3. United States—History— Revolution, 1775-1783—Biography—Juvenile literature. 4. Soldiers—South Carolina— Biography—Juvenile literature. 5. Soldiers—United States—Biography—Juvenile literature. 6. South Carolina. Militia—Biography—Juvenile literature. 7. South Carolina—History—Revolution, 1775-1783—Campaigns—Juvenile literature. 8. United States—History— Revolution, 1775-1783—Campaigns—Juvenile literature. I. Title.
E263.S7Z45 2010 975.7'03092—dc22
[B]
2010004674

BACKCOUNTRY FURY

CHARACTERS

Barrum Bobo — A neighbor and best friend to Thomas Young.

Christopher Brandon — A cousin and mess mate to Thomas Young.

Colonel Thomas Brandon — Thomas Young's uncle and militia co-commander.

Jim Collins — Thomas Young's mischievous messmate.

General Charles Cornwallis — The British commander of the southern campaign.

Bill Cunningham — A South Carolina loyalist militia major. This blood-thirsty backcountry Tory was often referred to as "Bloody Bill."

James Dillard — An officer in Thomas Young's regiment and husband to Mary Dillard.

Mary Ramage Dillard — A beautiful woman and friend of Thomas Young. She accompanied her husband into the militia.

General Nathaniel Greene — The American Patriot commander of the southern campaign.

Joseph Hayes — Replaced Colonel James Williams as co-commander of Thomas Young's militia regiment.

Lettie Hughes — The girl who tends to Thomas Young when he is in need.

Benjamin Jolly — Captain of Thomas Young's Carlisle Company.

James Kelly — A local Tory who knows Thomas Young.

Squire Kennedy — A distant relative of Thomas Young and father of William Kennedy.

Tony Zeiss

William Kennedy — A messmate and distant relative to Thomas Young.

Joe Kerr — A disabled teen who is an effective spy for the Partisans.

Captain George Littlefield — A local Tory who wants to kill Thomas Young.

General Francis Marion — The famous low-country Partisan commander known as the "Swamp Fox."

General Daniel Morgan — The famous Continental commander of the American forces at the Battle of Cowpens.

Adam Steedham — The vile Tory informant who helped Bloody Bill Cunningham attack Colonel Brandon and his militia regiment.

General Thomas Sumter — The famous central-South Carolina Militia commander known as the "Gamecock."

Lieutenant Colonel Banastre Tarleton — General Cornwallis's ambitious and blood-thirsty subordinate.

Henry Allen Tate — Thomas Young's Sergeant.

General George Washington — Commander of the American Continental Army.

Colonel William Washington — An esteemed Continental cavalry officer.

Lieutenant Colonel James Williams — A neighbor and co-commander of Thomas Young's regiment.

Daniel Williams — Colonel Williams' son and a friend of Thomas Young.

Joseph Williams — Colonel Williams' younger son and friend of Thomas Young.

Thomas Young — A sixteen-year-old patriot from upstate South Carolina.

Acknowledgments

I am grateful to my wife, Beth, for her support of this project and for walking through woods, streams, and cemeteries with me while researching the historical background for this book. I must next thank Allen Tate, the wonderful friend who intrigued me with his stories about the Southern Campaigns of the Revolutionary War. Charles Baxley, whose knowledge of the Southern Campaign is exceeded only by his passion for it, was a terrific mentor for this work as was my creative friend, Barry Weitz. Finally, I thank the late Joe C. M. Goldsmith, a well-known advocate for the Sons of the American Revolution, for his encouragement, support, and splendid tours in and around the Little River District. I dedicate this book to him.

Foreword

This book chronicles 18 months in the life of sixteen-year-old Thomas Young who lived and fought in South Carolina during America's revolution. All but one of the main characters were real people, however the dialog in most instances was created. The dialog is based on knowledge gleaned from their personal histories, memoirs, pension records, and from research about the significant Revolutionary War events in which they participated.

Thomas Young and his family and friends represent an exemplary display of sacrifice, courage, and determination in their pursuit of liberty for themselves and generations to follow.

The southern colonies during 1780 and 1781 were thrust into a civil war between those loyal to Great Britain and those who sought independence from the crown. No one could straddle the fence on this fundamental issue. People lived in an environment of neighbor against neighbor, congregation against congregation, and sometimes brother against brother. It is against this backdrop that Thomas Young made his decision to fight for the liberation of his new country, the United States of America.

The southern campaign of the Revolutionary War has been under emphasized by historical writers and it is hoped this work will help readers, especially young ones, develop a greater appreciation for the southern Partisans in particular and for all Patriots in general.

Tony Zeiss

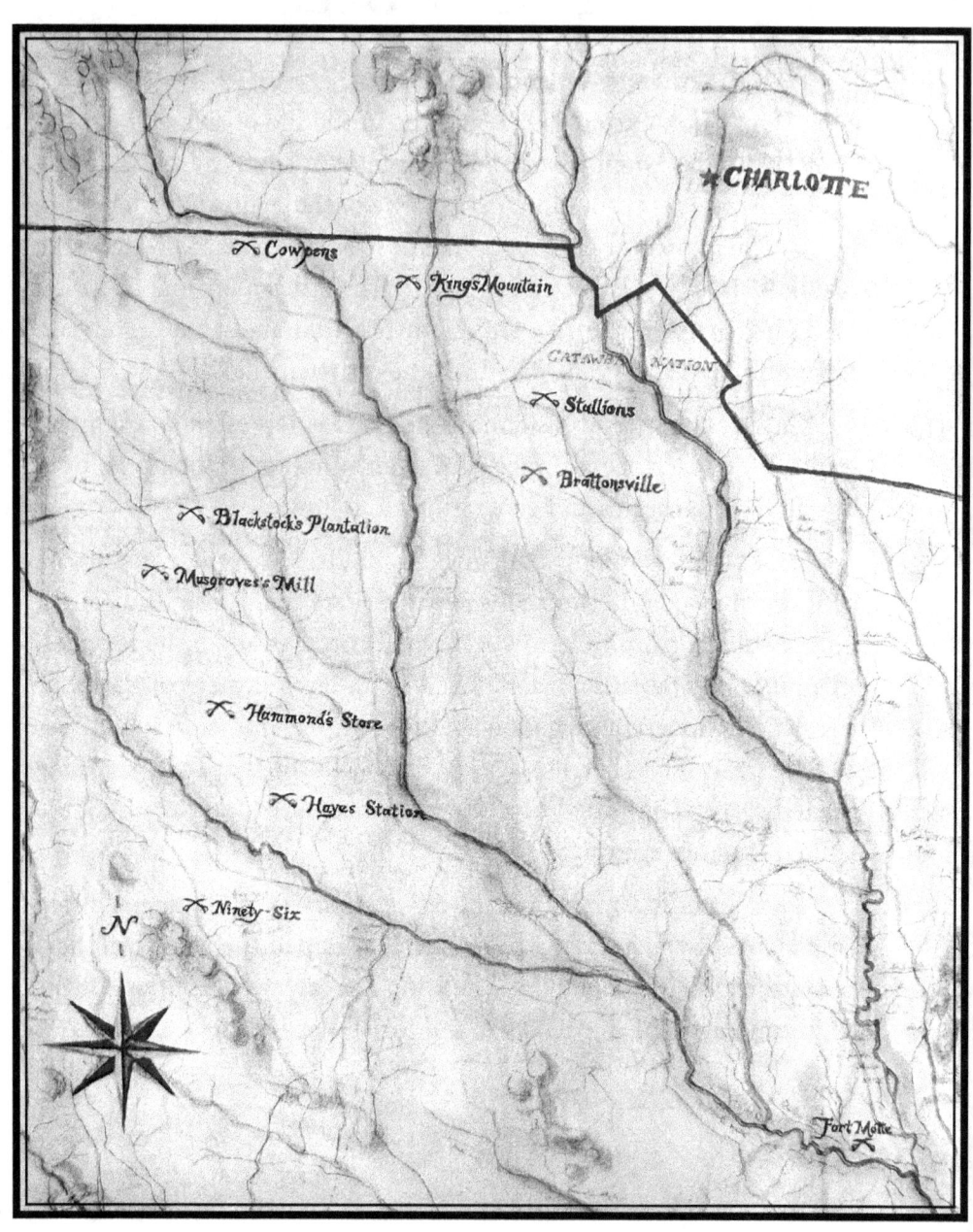

A Gathering Storm

May 1780

"Thomas, Thomas. Come quick!" From my mother's urgent plea, I knew something was terribly wrong. I dropped the harness I'd been stitching and ran from our barn toward the house. Mother wailed with a piercing moan I'd never heard before. I thought she must be dying. Uncle Thomas held her tightly to himself on the front porch. My sisters, Jane and Elizabeth, and my little brother, Andrew, clung to each other.

My sixteen-year-old heart leaped in my breast and a lump swelled in my throat as I ran as fast as I could toward the house. With Uncle Thomas being there, something must have happened to my father or my brother, John. Both of them had been off with the Militia commanded in part by Uncle Thomas. The Partisan Militia provided the only protection we had from the marauding Tories.

As I bounded up on the porch, Mother broke from Uncle Thomas' embrace and squeezed me tighter than ever before and sobbed. Then she gasped, "He's dead, Thomas. John is dead. They've killed my John."

"Bloody Bill Cunningham and his murdering bunch did it," my uncle said. Tears of grief and anger swelled in my eyes and overflowed as I tried to make sense of the situation. My heart pounded and my stomach felt wretched. Mother whimpered softly and I helped her sit on a chair. Elizabeth and Andrew sat down on the porch floor on either side of her, leaning on her legs. Jane brought her a clay mug full of water and a handkerchief. Everyone was crying, even my uncle and me.

Uncle Thomas continued, "We were camped near the Fairforest community when the Tories surrounded us and attacked … just before sunrise. They'd been tipped off by that turncoat Adam Steedham."

"But what happened to John?" I asked.

"He was on sentry duty and discovered them sneaking up through the woods. Most of us were still sleeping when he gave the shout of alarm."

"How was he killed?"

"He fired the first shot, drawing their attention. By the time we grabbed our rifles, Cunningham's men fired back and John fell, along with two others. We fought the best we could for about ten minutes, but they outnumbered us three to one. We retreated through a ravine."

Everything seemed unreal to me. It was like I was dreaming this dreadful thing, like I was detached from it all, but yet I knew it was real. I couldn't soak it all in. Uncle Thomas then turned to my mother. "William will be bringing in his body soon, Sis. They're coming by wagon."

"Oh my William. Is he okay? Is he all right?"

"Yes, Catherine. He's just fine. He'll be here soon."

Everything came at me too fast. My father was fine, but my brother was dead … gone forever. All the blood in my body rushed to my head and I could hardly breathe. They'd killed my big brother, John. He was my best friend in the world. I tore off my shirt, threw it in the dust, and swore an oath. "I'll kill Adam Steedham and Bill Cunningham if it's the last thing I ever do!"

After that proclamation, I needed to be alone … alone to try to sort it all out. Tears streamed over my cheeks and I didn't even try to hide them. I walked back to the barn and Red, John's lanky coon hound, followed me, nudging my leg as we walked. I scratched his tick-laden ears from habit and pulled off all I could find. I mashed them between my thumbnails and poor Red's blood burst out of the buggers pretty good. Then I climbed up the ladder to the hay loft where the sweet smelling hay overpowered every other odor in the barn. Red lay down by the ladder and whined just as if he knew John was gone. Dogs and horses seem to have a sixth sense about such things.

I sat near the open door right where John and I had worked side by side loading hay in the loft two or three times a season for many years. Of course, he could stack more hay than me since he was a full six feet tall and stronger. At age eighteen, he was a man now. But I'd just had a growth spurt and nearly caught up with him in height and strength.

I reclined on some of the fresh hay we'd put up just a couple of weeks back. John probably placed it here himself, I thought. He can't be gone, I kept thinking over and over. I could hear his voice and remembered his words the last time we spoke.

"I love you, Mother," he said just before returning to his militia camp. "Don't worry about Father and me. We Young's are pretty tough. Even Thomas is getting some impressive muscles." He stepped over and gave me a knuckle rub on my shaggy head. "You keep growing like you did this spring and I'll have to tie a brick on your head, boy. Can't have a younger brother getting taller than me, you know." Then we Indian-wrestled as brothers do. We grabbed hold of our right hands and pulled and pushed each other to see who fell to the ground first. John won, but I nearly bested him.

John always teased and wrestled with me like that and I loved him for it. It seems like he was happy all the time, too. And he taught me so much, like how to fish and hunt, and mend harnesses. He schooled me on girls and about how they were different from us, but different in a good way, mostly. Of course, I didn't have much confidence in being able to attract girls.

Just a month earlier at our Presbyterian meeting house pitch-in dinner, Patsy Lynch kept smiling at me from across the green. She was pretty, had curly blonde hair, and flashed bright blue eyes. All of us boys cottoned to her. I finally worked up the courage to smile back and conjured up the nerve to walk over her way. The closer I got to her, the dryer my mouth became and the palms of my hands sweated. I kept trying to swallow, but it wouldn't work. My legs felt like they were walking through molasses and I was afraid I must look like a darn fool. What if the other boys were watching? I sweated like a work horse in July.

"Hey, Patsy. How's that dew berry pie?" Everything went smooth until my voice cracked and the word pie squeaked out and sounded more like a Blue Jay's distress call than a human voice. I had tried to sound manly, but my adolescent voice gave me away. Patsy burst out laughing and I made a red-faced and hasty exit. I haven't wanted much to do with girls since then and maybe never. Things like that never happened to John. All the girls seemed to like him.

I spent the next hour or so trying to recollect every fond memory of my big brother and I resolved to remember them often so he'd always be alive in my mind. When I closed my eyes, I could see him clearly with his dark brown hair and handsome face. It made me proud that everyone said we looked just alike.

I shouldn't have been so surprised about John's death. I knew full well the War of the Revolution was about to erupt in upstate South Carolina where we lived. I knew it as well as I knew my name was Thomas Young.

Just last month, the British took Charleston and captured the entire Continental army of the south. They now marched toward the backcountry and the up state area where we lived. Our small plantation was located in the Little River District south of Spartanburg, South Carolina, just off a public road that connected the North Carolina Mountains down through South Carolina to Augusta, Georgia. This road was built on an original Cherokee path and was the main artery for commerce for everyone in the upstate area. Our plantation rested between the Tyger and Enoree Rivers.

Life was mostly hard work, but peaceful until the Cherokees began killing settlers and burning down their houses. That was about 1760, before I was born. There was a fortification called a block-house built down the road a piece at Hayes' station to help protect the people from the Indians.

After the settlers were victorious over the Cherokees, everything was peaceful again until people began to argue over being taxed by the British Parliament without any say in the matter. "Taxation without representation" was the phrase mostly heard in my home and at the meeting house.

My father didn't like the fact that the British military occupied Boston, the great seaport city, and he was always talking about how they murdered innocent civilians. He called it the Boston Massacre. Our neighbor, James Williams, a member of the South Carolina Provincial Assembly, our local grist mill owner, and now a Colonel in the Partisan mounted militia, cautioned people about saying such seditious things in public. That's when the men, including my father and brother John, began assembling in secret at the meeting house.

In May 1775, word came that the British Regulars had marched on the villages of Lexington and Concord up in Massachusetts. They fired upon the locals at Lexington and killed several on the town green. This atrocity fired up patriotism across the colonies. Over in Mecklenburg County in North Carolina they declared their independence from the Crown a full year before the Continental Congress did the same.

There was great unrest in our part of the country since we had no law enforcement or protection and the only order to things came from whoever was the strongest. The Tories, who were loyal to the King, and the Whigs, who preferred to be called Partisans or Patriots, began fighting each other in an organized way at Fort Ninety Six, south of us, as early as November 1775. But we hadn't experienced any real fighting in our area until now.

After capturing Charleston, General Clinton issued an edict that anyone who wouldn't declare loyalty to the king would be labeled a rebel and be treated as an enemy to the crown. This pronouncement created an immediate division between neighbors and even brothers. And Clinton's successor, General Charles Cornwallis, was now carrying out the edict with vigor.

You didn't know whom to trust. A man might pretend to be a Partisan only to turn up later as a Tory spy. No one in the back-country, including the upstate district, wore a uniform and Tories and Partisans all looked the same.

I continued to muse about these things, trying to understand what led to John's death, when Uncle Thomas called to me and said my father was coming up the road with John's body in the wagon.

I couldn't wait to see my father's tall sinewy frame to be sure he was unharmed, but I dreaded seeing John's body. I felt guilty about this, but I didn't want to carry an image of his lifeless form in my head for the rest of my life.

Uncle Thomas stayed around until we held a proper burial for John. Our preacher conducted the service and went on and on about how John was a fine young man. Deacon Jolly talked about John's courage and my father quoted scripture. I believed myself to be a man, but I cried and cried at John's funeral. I couldn't help myself and I wasn't ashamed of it at all. Every person there cried over poor John.

About everyone in the immediate area, except those off chasing Tories, stood there at the grave site in the Duncan Church Presbyterian Meeting House Cemetery. Uncle Thomas's family, who lived miles away, couldn't get there because it was now too dangerous to travel without armed guards. And we couldn't wait too long to bury John. Uncle Thomas and most of the men had to get back to their militia camp before Cunningham and his Tories made another raid. All the men in attendance, except for Hank and the field hands, were armed in case of another ambush.

Red howled mournfully every now and then from our barn where we'd tied him up. A cool breeze carried the dog's howls across the fields. He must have been almost a mile away. That was the saddest sound I ever heard.

They buried John in his hunting shirt and breeches, but without his shoes. Shoes were hard to come by and I'd outgrown my only pair. I'd cut off the toe ends to make more room.

"Thomas," my mother said as she handed his shoes to me, "these will be your shoes now." I'd always been proud to wear John's hand-me-downs, but I had mixed emotions about those shoes. I felt bad about him being buried without them and I had concerns whether I could fill his shoes, live up to his standards.

After things quieted down and everyone left our place, Mother stayed in her room and cried and my father did his best to get the family through this tragedy. Without being told, my sister Jane, who was seventeen, pretty, and 'coming into bloom', my father said, assumed the cooking and cleaning responsibilities. Elizabeth, who was fourteen, gangly, but dimply cute, assumed most of the other household chores, like washing clothes and such, normally done by my mother. I was proud of them. Even little Andrew, who just celebrated his eighth birthday, seemed more mature. He wasn't demanding attention or whining like he usually did. Everyone grew up a great deal during those hard days.

I knew what I had to do.

All of us sat around the kitchen table after supper when I decided to broach the subject. Mother was thin in stature, but she seemed especially frail and I worried about her reaction the most. Nevertheless, I shoved my fingers through my combed back dark hair and spoke up. I turned to my uncle who was only of average height, but was exceptionally strong. He was a natural leader and very articulate, my mother said. I was as proud of him as I was John and my father.

"Uncle Thomas, I want to go back with you and join your regiment."

"Oh no, Thomas," my mother put her hands to her cheeks. "I simply couldn't stand losing another son." She pulled out her handkerchief and daubed her eyes, but I remained resolute.

"I've stayed home as you've asked long enough." "You're just a boy."

"I'm not a boy and haven't been for some time now. I mean no disrespect, but there are plenty of men young as me who are fighting already."

My father intervened. "Now, now, Catherine, don't you see he has to go? He's clear headed and he can shoot better than men twice his age."

Mother knew he was right and I guess she knew she couldn't keep me from joining up. I'd sworn to avenge John's death. I put on my stubborn face and didn't blink an eye. She looked at my father, sighed, and bit her lip.

"Uncle Thomas, I'd like to fight with John's friends. I figure you'll catch Bloody Bill and that stinking Steedham and I want to be there when that happens."

Uncle Thomas leaned across the table toward my father. "William, how do you feel about it?"

"He's your namesake, Thomas. If that's where he'd like to be, I reckon that's where he ought to be. And I'll be nearby most of the time since we generally all stay in the same camp." My father was a company captain under Uncle Thomas. Everyone had confidence in Uncle Thomas.

"Private Young," Uncle Thomas smiled at me, "gather your weapons and accouterments, a change of clothes, your sleeping blanket, and get your best horse. We'll leave within the hour."

I jumped up and saluted. "Yes, sir, Colonel Brandon."

That's when Jane, Elizabeth, and Andrew surrounded me, hugged and kissed me, and implored me to be careful. I hugged my mother and told her I would be fine and that I would make them pay for John. She cried softly. After shaking hands with my father and thanking him, I went upstairs to gather my things. Hundreds of thoughts flew through my mind and I couldn't concentrate on any one of them for long.

I gathered my Lindsey Woolsey coat, an extra hunting shirt, and two pair of socks. In my haversack, I added my flint and steel pouch, my flint wallet, my bullet mold, some linen strips for wadding, a tin of bear grease for the wadding patches, and my bag of lead rifle balls. I grabbed my rifle, my most prized possession, and Andrew brought me a gourd canteen covered with deer hide. I pulled on my canvas leggings over my trousers, threw on my black floppy hat, picked up my knife, and hurried downstairs. John's shoes fit me well.

We saddled up and were ready to go when my father handed me my small Bible which I hadn't thought about taking. "It'll bring you more comfort than you know, Son. Just remember Paul's advice in his second letter to the Corinthian church. He said the Lord is Spirit and where the Spirit of the Lord is, there is Liberty." Father was always quoting the Bible.

"That's the cause we're fighting for, Thomas, liberty," Uncle Thomas added. "And Catherine, you can believe two things. We'll even the score for John and we'll win the cause…we'll have our liberty." He then began loading his rifle. "Load up that rifle, Thomas, we can't be too careful, you know."

I poured a measure of powder down the barrel, rammed down a greased patch of linen wrapped around a lead ball, and poured some powder in the pan of my flintlock. Then I leaned down and kissed my mother's teary cheek and she hugged me for an embarrassingly long time. I told her I loved her, shook my father's strong, weathered hand again, and said goodbye to my sisters and my little brother.

"You won't let nothing happen to you, will ya Thomas? You're my only brother now."

"Of course not. Don't even worry about it. But you'll have to help Mother out more than usual since I'll be gone. Can you do that?"

"Yes."

"And you'll have to take care of Red now that I'm gone. He's old and needs to be fed at least once a day. And take the ticks off his ears every day. John and I will both be pleased with you."

Mother said, "He'll be the man of the house now that both you and your father will be away, won't you, Andrew?" She wiped a handkerchief at her eyes.

"Yep."

I tousled his blond hair.

"I'll join you in a week," my father said.

We mounted our horses and rode north, up the old Ninety Six Road. I felt perfectly confident in my favorite horse I named Dot. She was a sorrel-colored mare with a white dot on her forehead. She loved apples and sugar candy and was more loyal than a dog. We rode for about a mile on that dirt road through the rolling, wooded hills without speaking. At first I was very alert, thinking about Bloody Bill Cunningham and his men riding freely about. But it was a comfortable ride and the clop clopping of the horses hooves on the packed dirt road soothed me. Still, I couldn't get John out of my mind. Uncle Thomas must have sensed it because he broke the silence. "I'm real sorry about John. I know how close you two were."

"It's not right. John was so perfect in woodcraft and such a fine athlete. How could anyone get the jump on him?"

"They slipped up on foot just before daylight. We'd had a rain and everything was wet. It was easy for them to walk in quietly. And every slight breeze shook the rain off the tree leaves which helped conceal their approach, most likely. It just proves even the best of us can be surprised. You'll do well to remember this."

"I really miss him already."

"Of course you do. You two were more like twins than brothers with two year's difference between you. Your mother always said you were like two peas in a pod."

A few minutes later, Uncle Thomas asked, "What was the favorite thing you liked about John?"

"I liked the way he kidded around … the way he teased me and taught me things."

"Like what?"

"Like when he first took me quail hunting. When Red flash-pointed the first covey, birds whirled off in all directions and I couldn't decide which one to aim at. I ended up shooting at the whole covey, hoping to hit one, but missed entirely. John grinned and said, 'It's the mark of a beginner. Remember to stay calm and aim at only one bird at a time.' He let that sink in, and said, 'Quail hunting is like everything else in life. Try to think before acting.

That next Sunday, to my embarrassment, he called me the 'covey shooter' in front of all our friends at our meeting house. He didn't have to repeat that lesson, I can tell you."

"I expect all of us learned that lesson the hard way … even John.

What else did you like about him?"

I lifted my hat and glided my fingers through my hair as I thought about his question. "I always knew he was there for me. If we'd get in trouble, he took the blame. And he'd take the first whacks from father's belt whenever it came to that."

Uncle Thomas twisted in his saddle and looked at me. "Those are mighty good qualities for a brother. He treated his militia mates the same way."

"I'm not surprised. Everybody liked him. I hope I can help take his place in some way."

"That's a fine idea. I'll assign you to his old mess. Just be smart and don't take any chances. You're as good as John in shooting and you have his instincts, but always be on your guard. The family, especially your mother, couldn't take any more grief."

We rode the rest of the way talking about family things and the militia. After Cunningham's raid, Uncle Thomas had given orders to move the camp northeast to the far side of the Broad River. We rode for another couple of hours, crossed the Broad River at a ford, and I began to smell wood smoke. Uncle Thomas said he hoped Aunt Elizabeth would let their son, Christopher, join us. We rounded a bend and saw the wood smoke from the militia camp's cooking fires. The thin trails of smoke drifted up through pine trees in the fading sunlight. My heart rate increased as I realized I was going to be a part of it all and I felt ten feet tall. I couldn't wait to get a chance to even the score with Steedham and Cunningham.

LEARNING THE ROPES

As we neared the regimental militia camp, I could hardly believe my eyes. Small campfires flickered all over the top of a hardwood ridge with pine trees mixed in here and there. Almost two hundred men camped here. A sentry stopped us, but immediately recognized Uncle Thomas. After being told all was well, we rode into the camp. My cousin Christopher, Uncle Thomas's son, walked up and grabbed the reins of his father's horse.

"Hey there, Father. Hey, Thomas."

"Guess your mother finally decided you could join us?" Colonel Brandon said.

"After we heard about John, I told her I had to join up. She relented and sends this letter to you." Christopher pulled it out of his hunting shirt and handed it to Uncle Thomas.

He took the letter and slid it into his shirt next to his breast. "You and Thomas will be good for each other. I'll assign you to the same mess unit. Just do your best and remember who you are. We family members have to set the example, you know."

"I just want to make you proud," Christopher said. "You've done that by being here."

I slapped Christopher on the back and he did the same to me. We were the same age and always got along fine at family gatherings and such. Much like his father, he was average in stature, but had the courage of a cornered bobcat. He was light complexioned with red hair like his father's and if he ever thought someone disrespected him, he would tear into them without hesitation. I admired his pluck. We agreed to share the same tent and spent the evening discussing our new condition. We couldn't wait to learn the ways of soldiering and to get an opportunity to avenge John's death. And we wanted to prove ourselves worthy to our fathers.

The other members of our mess were on a patrol assignment and would return by daybreak. We were on our own, but most everyone our age knew how to get along in a camp. First, we piled up a foot or more of dead pine needles for mattresses and put our blankets down. We wouldn't get a tent until the next day, but sleeping in the open was more fun if it didn't rain. My pine needle pallet was just as comfortable as my bed at home, but the mosquitoes and woods creatures pestered me much more. The blood-sucking ticks were a nuisance, but we could see them and they'd back out of your skin when you held a fire brand next to them. It burnt some, but it was better than leaving them there with their heads stuck in you. If you tried to pull them off, their heads would pop off inside your skin and cause a fester. But ticks were mild compared to chiggers, red bugs we called them, and lice. These tiny critters made me scratch more than old Red.

I don't think I slept a wink that night. If I wasn't itching and scratching, a darned ole owl screeched about every time I began to slumber. If you have ever heard a screech owl, you know how it can unnerve you, especially knowing you can come under attack by the Tories any minute. But I never let on that anything kept me awake.

I thought about John most of the night and finally concluded that, in a way, John's spirit could stay alive by living through me. In everything I did after this night, I tried to ask myself what John would do in the same circumstance. I knew I had to learn to grow up in a hurry. Oh, I could put up a manly impression, but deep down I was plenty concerned about whether I could cut the mustard and whether I would fit in with grownups in the militia.

At sunup, Captain Benjamin Jolly, our company commander and a deacon from our meeting house, introduced us to a small mess unit of two other men to cook and share meals together. I had always liked Deacon Jolly. He was in his late twenties and still single. My father said he worked hard at everything he did. I liked him because he never acted like he was better than anyone else and he liked to work with teenagers.

To our delight, an older shirttail cousin to both of us, William

Kennedy, was in our mess. He had served in the militia for almost two years and we looked up to him for this. I noticed that I'd grown taller than him, but he was more filled out. He wore his brown hair long, like most of us, and tied it off in the back.

"Sit down boys, and have some corn pone. It's not your mother's recipe, but after awhile anything hot tastes good out here." We sat on the logs that had been assembled around the cook fire. "From the looks of ya, you could stand some fattening up." He was frying the corn mixture over an open fire in an iron skillet with some butter, just like Mother fixed flap jacks. They smelled heavenly. The fire had two wrought iron rods stuck into the ground on either side of it. A small iron spit bar lay across the iron rods. A tin tea pail and an iron soup pot hung from this horizontal bar. It wasn't as fancy as my mother's set up back home, but it worked well. William flipped the corn cakes one last time, glanced at me and said, "We're all sorry about John, Thomas."

"Thanks."

"He was a great friend and a braver man never fought for liberty."

"He's the main reason I'm here." I picked up a pine cone and threw it at a nearby tree. "They'll be sorry for what they did."

"You'll get plenty of chances to make 'em pay, but don't forget we're fighting for liberty, not revenge. Revenge is nice, but it can make you take risks you shouldn't take. Out here you learn to think before acting or you'll make the mistake of your life."

"Sounds like something John would say," I said.

We introduced ourselves to another veteran named James Collins from the New Acquisition District, about fifty miles northeast of my home place. We knew of him from neighborhood gatherings like the annual harvest festivals. He stood well over six feet tall, was skinny as a rail, and his nose was crooked, like it had been broken and didn't heal back straight. He had dirty blond hair and a colorful personality. He lived with his grandmother who had a relative or two here in the upstate. It seemed like most everybody in the upstate was related to each other in some way.

William served the corn flapjacks. "There you go, boys. Eat 'em up 'cause you never know when you might get your next vittles. You're in the militia now and nothing runs on a regular schedule."

"You can say that again," said Collins. "It's hurry up and wait.

Then it's wait, but hurry up."

"Oh don't be so negative, Collins," William replied. "You'll be discouraging these new recruits. It's fun being out here. How else could you get away from the farm work to camp out with your friends and enjoy God's creation?"

"Like puttin' up with all these redbugs and skeeters is fun?" Collins said, scratching himself.

"There you go again, trying to discourage these new men. Don't pay this grouch no never mind. He never grew up proper."

"Don't be disrespecting my grandmother, William."

"I do apologize, Mr. Collins." William turned back to us. "The real reason he's so disagreeable is that he's been out here on this foray too long and he's missing his sweetheart … makes him kind of moody."

"There's sure enough some truth in that, William. Leastwise I'm handsome enough to have a sweetheart. Her name is Alexandra Hazel and her raven hair and radiant face make her the most beautiful young woman in the backcountry." Collins sneered straight at William, but the crooked end of his nose pointed off to the left. William pitched Collins a corn dodger straight from the frying pan and it landed in his lap.

"Ow! That's hot!" Collins said. He threw the dodger into his wooden bowl. "Your only problem is you were born ugly and backslid from there."

"Look who's talking," William said. "Boys, have you ever seen a nose more crooked than his?"

"Lay off my nose. It's what makes me distinctive," he flashed a toothy grin.

I liked these men and their friendly bantering. I also couldn't wait to learn how to be the best soldier possible. Mostly I wanted to learn to be a great soldier so I could kill as many Tories as possible and Bill Cunningham and Adam Steedham in particular.

To my great delight, William served Black English tea to help us wash down the corn pone. Tea was the one pleasurable thing that everyone in the backcountry valued highly. And William was right. That corn pone tasted mighty fine out there in the piney woods.

"Thomas, since you and Christopher are the newest members of this mess, you get the privilege of tending to the latrine. Its smelly work, but it builds character," William said.

"Thanks for the honor," I said. "We'll keep fresh holes dug, as long as everyone covers them when they finish their constitution."

"You boys will also have to keep us stacked high in firewood. Collins and I will cook the meals." This sounded like a fine proposition to me. I knew next to nothing about cooking since my mother and sisters tended to that work.

A half hour later, the veteran troops went off to drill in a large field, company by company. Christopher and I walked to a smaller field to join about four other new recruits who had been assigned to Captain Jolly's Company. My best friend and neighbor, Barrum Bobo, a year older than Christopher and me, was among these new recruits. He stood a few inches shorter than me, but was more muscular. He looked sort of rugged, especially with that long black hair. We were pleased to see him and invited him to join our mess.

Ben Hollingsworth, also a member of our Duncan Creek Presbyterian meeting house, was the lieutenant in charge of new recruits. The British Crown wouldn't let us call our meeting house a church. The Crown recognized only the Church of England as being legitimate. Parliament wouldn't even recognize weddings performed outside of their official Church. Of course we held our own weddings anyway and if an Anglican preacher came around trying to convert us, the men, often led by Mr. Hollingsworth, ran him off by sicking their dogs on him.

My mother said Hollingsworth was a fine Christian, but he'd been "churched" a number of times for imbibing too much in strong liquor. The elders would have to visit him and he'd repent, promising to change his bad habit, but he'd sooner or later yield to that liquid tempter again. Father said he'd die of "barrel fever" if he didn't quit drinking so much from the whiskey barrel. My mother said he needed a wife to whip him into shape. Hollingsworth also butchered the Kings English pretty well with his thick Scottish accent. He was a large, barrel-chested man with graying hair. Christopher didn't know him, but Bobo and I assured him Hollingsworth was a good and kindly man in spite of his unsavory habits. He served as our induction officer and instructor.

"He sure is brandy-faced, ain't he," Christopher said. Hollingsworth heard him. "Shush up and no speaking when

I'm talking. Form a line and put up ye right hands, boys," Hollingsworth commanded. He pulled out a tattered piece of paper and read, "Repeat after me: I, state your full name, swear total allegiance to the cause of liberty, and swear to uphold the commands and authority of my militia unit, and to protect all who love liberty by any means within my power, so help me God." We dutifully and proudly repeated the oath.

"You're in the militia now, men. Leave your boyhood ways behind ye. In this army, every man depends upon and protects every other man. There's nary room for foolishness or laziness. We've gotta work together and function as a team if we expect to stay alive and win our independence."

Hollingsworth turned the paper over with his stubby fingers and continued, "Every man in this militia is a volunteer, just like you. They range in age from ten to fifty and they're all sacrificing to make this country a better and safer place, free of tyranny, taxation, and an unjust government. This cause is greater than any of us and is certainly more important than any one of you young pups." The rotund lieutenant looked at each of us with penetrating eyes that caused shivers to run up my spine. Evidently serving in the militia takes away some of your kindness, I reasoned.

"Men, in case there's any doubt, you are troops serving in the Fairforest District commanded by Colonel Thomas Brandon. You're assigned to the Little River Regiment which includes the Carlisle Company led by Captain Benjamin Jolly. This regiment also includes the Antrim, Belfast, and Duncan companies. Of course, you know your daddy is captain of the Duncan Company, Thomas." Hollingsworth nodded to me, but didn't smile a bit. "Our regiment is closely aligned with Colonel James Williams and his Ninety Six District militia and we often fight together when we need a larger force. When we join together, Colonel Williams is the ranking officer.

"You'll obey the officers of this command, specifically Captain Jolly, me, and Sergeant Tate. You'll serve when called and for as long as it takes to achieve our cause. Your first enlistment is for thirty days. That'll no doubt be repeated for more times than you have fingers and toes. We'll attempt to release you during planting and harvest times, but there's no guarantee of such privileges. You will receive your pay whenever the South Carolina leaders send it. Do ye understand?"

"Yes, sir," we replied with straight backs and eyes forward.

"Furthermore, there'll be no leaving the camp without permission, no fightin' with each other, and no stealin' food nor drink from people unless they're Tories. Anyone who breaks these rules or is insubordinate to a man of superior rank will be severely disciplined. Do ye understand?"

We answered in the affirmative.

"Good. Now, Sergeant Tate, teach these green peas the fine art of drilling on the field."

And that's the way it all began. We drilled on foot, which didn't make much sense to me since we mounted militiamen were most always on horseback. We more or less learned how to respond to the basic foot marching commands until noon. It was hot, sweaty, and sometimes confusing work. Sergeant Tate shouted at us when we made a wrong turn, which was mighty often. Finally, we took a short break for a skimpy meal of oats mush with no butter or salt and some hard bread. We sat under a huge white oak and ate the mush out of gourds with our fingers. That was the last time we ever left our wooden spoons back at the camp.

"This mush would choke a goat!" Christopher said. "At least they're feeding us," I said.

"I hope there's an improvement for supper," Christopher said.

"And to think I'm doing this mostly to impress girls." Bobo winked. "I'm beginning to wonder what I've gotten myself into." He stretched out his solid frame on the grass, interlocked his fingers behind his black-haired head, and closed his eyes.

"You're always thinking about girls," I said.

"It comes natural because of my French blood I recon," Bobo responded.

"Bobo is French?" I asked.

"Through and through," Bobo said. "Our name was originally spelled B-e-a-u b-e-a-u."

"Nevertheless, you'd better start thinking about Tories and how to protect your sorry hide," I told him. I guess some girls would find him to be handsome, but he hadn't been able to spark any yet that I knew of. For that matter, neither had I.

In the afternoon, we marched for about five miles and drilled some more until evening. Then we set up the tent that had been requisitioned. Luckily, it was big enough for the three of us. We had a devil of a time figuring out how to set it up, but we managed it just before nightfall.

Over the next two weeks we learned when, who, and how to salute and how to load and reload our rifles faster than ever before especially when they issued us pre-packaged cartridges of powder, wadding, and bullets for our muskets and rifles. Unfortunately, getting those cartridges was a rare circumstance. We practiced how to load and shoot from various positions.

I wasn't sure if I liked our Sergeant. His name was Henry Allen Tate and he came from over east from his father's plantation on Buffalo Creek near the Broad River. He had a wiry frame and appeared to be plenty tough. We learned that he preferred his friends call him Allen, but we called him Sergeant, of course. I did fancy his red floppy hat since most of us wore black or brown ones. Outside of that, I didn't find too much about him to admire. Seemed like he was always bossing us around and we could never please him. And he drilled us much longer than all the other units. Nothing is more boring than foot drills. Drilling with horses was a different matter. It was more sensible and respectable, I reasoned. And it was generally fun.

After cleaning our wooden bowls and spoons with water and sand, my messmates and I sat around the fire most evenings singing songs, playing cards, or just talking.

"You think we really have a chance to beat the British?" Bobo asked.

"Hell yes," Christopher said.

"I don't think we have any choice in the matter now. We have to win or we'll lose everything," I said. "And we're making some headway. Look at North Carolina. They ran that British Governor Martin out of the Tryon Palace over there in New Bern and set up their own provincial assembly."

"That's perfectly appropriate," Christopher said. "I hope we can run them out of Charleston and take back our capital."

"How about we run them out of the backcountry first," Collins said.

"That's right," William said. He sat in his usual place reclining against a beech tree smoking and drinking hot tea. He exhaled from his burl wood pipe and blew two perfect smoke circles. "What we need is a big victory over British troops. That would stop so many backcountry men from becoming Tories. My father says most people are really fence-sitters waiting to see who will most likely win before joining one side or the other."

William's tobacco smelled sweet and had a soothing effect on me. I tried smoking a pipe once, but I discovered it smelled much better than it tasted. Besides, my father said it wasn't good for the lungs. He'd quit smoking because of lung trouble.

"Let's play a little rummy, boys. It'll probably only cost you a pence or two, but you'll be learning from a master," Collins grinned as he deftly shifted his cards. Luckily, we played Gen Rummy at home all the time. Collins was a good player though and I lost a little coinage, but not much. Collins gleefully beat everyone and flashed that toothy grin whenever he won a pot. We played long into the night and I enjoyed it immensely.

However, I went to bed thinking about what it would be like to fight in a big battle and how good it would feel if I could kill Cunningham and Steedham. I created battle scenes in my mind, but it was somewhat difficult since I'd never been in a battle. I'd even picture myself riding home as a hero for having put those Tories in the earth.

The next morning my messmates and I decided to take a bath and boil our clothes down at the Broad River. It wasn't a large river, but there were some deep holes where the water changed course in broad, sweeping bends.

"It's high time we looked after ourselves," Bobo said. "These little critters are about to drive me insane."

"That's why we're boiling our clothes," William said. "It'll kill all the vermin."

"But don't forget to wash your heads with this lye soap," Collins added. "It's the only thing that'll kill head lice."

"Let's hope it'll take the stink off you," Christopher said. "Why do you say that, you little weasel?"

Christopher's face flushed and he glared at Collins.

"He only said what the rest of us were thinking," William laughed.

I didn't hear the rest of the conversation since Bobo and I dove into the cold pool of clear water. It felt magnificent and I found myself in a whole new world, a world of peace and serenity and coolness. Bobo swam buck naked like me. He looked odd with his dark-skinned face and arms and his lily-white torso and legs. I looked down and realized I looked the same. Then the rest of the boys jumped into the pool making great splashes and yelling like Indians.

"Stay down wind of me until you've soaped up good," Christopher told Collins.

Collins replied, "You're just jealous because you don't smell like a man yet."

"Ha. I'll bet that girl you've been talking about would agree with me."

"You don't know nothing about girls. They like manly men."

"Then you'd best be worrying some," Christopher said. Collins sneered and swam over to Christopher. "I'll learn you to shoot off your mouth." And he dunked Christopher good. He surfaced, sputtering and red-faced. He wailed his arms trying to hit Collins, but Collins held him off until he calmed down.

"Too bad we don't have some girls to go skinny dipping with," Bobo said.

"You're too young to be thinking such things," William said. "You don't know, Bobo," I said. "All he ever thinks about is girls."

"You're pretty much right about that," Bobo said. Truth be known, I spent a powerful amount of time thinking about them myself, but I'd always end up remembering my brush with Patsy Lynch. Then I'd ask myself what girl would want a skinny boy in his brother's shoes? I'd probably grow up to be like lieutenant Hollingworth … a rum-potted old bachelor.

After a wonderful respite in the river, we built a fire and boiled our clothes in an iron pot located there for that purpose. While waiting for the clothes, I noticed a number of small mouth bass slurping up some mayflies near an under-cut bank. I made a mental note to come back with a fishing pole sometime soon. Bobo didn't notice the fish, but kept talking about the fine red clay along the banks. He said it would make good chimney bricks. That's where we differed. Bobo thought about building things and making money and I thought about catching things and how good they'd taste for dinner.

The scorching sun dried our clothes and it was a relief being rid of the lice and ticks that plagued us night and day. Our trousers and hunting shirts smelled better too, but they were getting tattered some. Bobo and I dressed, then walked our horses down to the creek and let them cool off. They played around in that water like children.

That evening, Sergeant Tate assigned me to my first picket duty. Pickets, usually privates, were placed on the perimeter of the entire camp twenty-four hours a day as guards. Everyone dreaded night duty because it was the most dangerous and they lost a lot of sleep.

"Young, you're on picket duty tonight from sundown to midnight." It was my first night duty, however, and I sort of looked forward to it. Just before dark, he led me out from camp about a quarter mile along the old road. "Sit right here above the road and keep your eyes and ears open." I sat down and leaned against a beech tree. "And no sleeping or day dreaming. The whole regiment is depending upon you. Just like they depended upon your brother. If you do half as well as him, we'll be proud of you … only don't get yourself killed." He pointed out several clearings through the brush and cedar trees where I could see for half a mile or more.

"If someone comes up, ask for the password. If he doesn't return the right password, stop him."

"What if he won't stop?" "Then shoot him." "What's the password?"

"Tyger. And nobody passes without the password. Remember

that. You'll be relieved of duty around midnight. The quarter moon should be about straight up then." Sergeant Tate turned and walked toward the camp. "Stay awake and don't shoot your relief man."

Things got very quiet and lonely as the sky darkened and the birds quit chirping. At dusk I saw two does walk across the road. After that I heard that ole screech owl and way off to the north a wolf howled and another one answered. I wondered if they were coming my way. I couldn't build a fire to scare them off.

I pictured John as he would have been in the same circumstance. I knew he wouldn't have been scared of anything, especially owls and wolves. I wondered how he felt when he saw Bloody Bill Cunningham and his gang surrounding the camp that morning. I wondered what it felt like to be shot. I closed my eyes and could almost smell my brother. It wasn't a bad smell like rotten eggs or cow manure. It smelled kind of comforting, musky like. I determined that he was there with me, looking after me like he always did. I quit worrying about wild animals and concentrated on looking for the enemy. Our whole camp depended upon me.

Twenty minutes later full darkness set in and I heard strange sounds in the forest. Nothing looked the same as when I first sat down. I used all my will power to stay calm. Did something move out there across the road, or was it just the wind blowing the bushes?

I sat there, perfectly still except for swiveling my head a little. I looked and listened as hard as I could. That's when I glimpsed movement off to my left. Something flew straight for my head. I ducked from instinct and the missile missed me, but knocked my hat off. It flashed silently past me and rose out of sight. I put my hat back on and looked all about, but neither saw nor heard anything. Then it happened again, only this time I saw it coming for me. It was a large owl and he meant business. I ducked and he swooshed past me. An owl can kill a man if it hits him full speed and my nerves were on full alert. I couldn't understand why he was attacking me. I finally figured out the owl was seeing my white hatband moving around and probably had mistaken it for a rabbit's tail. I quickly removed the hatband and threw it under a juniper bush. If it drew an owl's attention, it could just as well draw the attention of a Tory.

About an hour later I had calmed down considerably and was embarrassed to admit I'd been scared out of my wits by an owl. That's when I heard the unmistakable sound of footsteps. Sounding vague at first, the soft steps became more distinct the closer they got. They grew louder. Someone was coming straight toward me. It wasn't even close to midnight so it couldn't be my replacement. It couldn't be Sergeant Tate, he wouldn't play such games. The footsteps got closer and closer and I could hear rocks and sticks crunching under each step.

"Stop. What's the password?" The footsteps kept coming. "What's the password? Sergeant Tate, is that you?" I raised my rifle and cocked the hammer. My heart beat hard enough to hear it.

"Stop or I will shoot!" The footsteps were no more than thirty feet away. What if it's a Tory … or an Indian? Most Indians don't speak English, but they've been fighting with the British and not too far from here.

I saw movement right in front of me. I pictured a tomahawk slashing through the air toward me. I aimed and squeezed the trigger.

The rifle flashed and nearly deafened me with its loud report. An awful noise erupted from my opponent and I heard a thud as he hit the ground. I jumped behind a large tree and reloaded as fast as possible. I listened for sounds, but heard only a slight flutter of leaves trembling in the wind.

After a few minutes I heard a couple of men running toward my position from the camp. "Tyger, Tyger," Sergeant Tate said.

"I'm over here. I shot someone, I think."

"What happened, Young? Are you all right?"

"I'm fine, Sergeant, but someone came up and wouldn't respond when I asked for the password. I asked for it three times, but he wouldn't answer and just kept coming so I shot."

"Show me where you last saw him." He turned to William. "Kennedy, stand guard here."

I led the sergeant through the brush to the spot where I'd last seen movement and there it lay.

"It's a horse! You've shot a horse, Young." William Kennedy ran over.

"Nice shooting, Thomas. You got him right between the eyes," Kennedy chided.

I wanted to die or at least hide under a rock. To my relief, Sergeant Tate didn't jump on me.

"It's mighty unfortunate for the horse, but you did the right thing, Young." He patted me on the back. Nevertheless, my stomach twisted into knots and I felt awful. I'd never been so embarrassed in my life. I'd been doing fairly well at fitting in with the seasoned men, then I had to do a durn fool thing like shooting a horse. I'd shamed Uncle Thomas and my family and I couldn't do a blessed thing about it. I wondered what John would do and I finally concluded he'd tough it out like a man. So that's what I did. I took the teasing and laughed about it with them.

It was good to laugh since we'd soon be shooting at the enemy, much sooner than any of us imagined, and there would be little to laugh about.

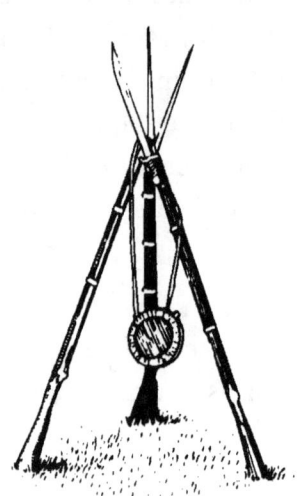

FIRST ENGAGEMENT

July 1780

The morning after the horse incident, my messmates and I took more target practice at the firing range.

"If Thomas shot a horse between the eyes in the dark, why does he need to practice?" Bobo asked Sergeant Tate.

"Yeah, it's nice knowing we've got such a good marksman in the company," Collins said. "I've never known a real horse killer before."

"Shush up and shoot. Young did the right thing out there last night," Tate said. I began to take a liking to the Sergeant.

"Ha," I replied to Collins "You'll be appreciating my accuracy when we start fighting Tories."

The boys taunted me for two weeks or more for shooting that horse, but even Colonel Williams told me he would have done the same thing and he believed it was a Tory horse anyway. And my father came over to our camp and spent an evening with me. He told me how he'd once shot a prize coon hound by mistake.

Much to our surprise, Lieutenant Hollingsworth and Sergeant Tate grew considerably nicer as the days went by and they gained more confidence in us. We all shot pretty well and I seldom missed the mark. We shot from a standing position, a kneeling position, and from lying down. Sergeant Tate called it the prone position. My rifle shot flat and true up to two hundred yards or more. I figured John would be proud of me. All of us messmates became good friends. It felt good to belong to a group of militiamen, especially William and Collins and other seasoned veterans. We hadn't yet proved ourselves worthy in battle, but Christopher, Bobo, and I were beginning to feel like real soldiers now and we were eager to go on our first patrol.

We didn't have long to wait. Later that week, I went on my first squad assignment with a small group of about ten men led by Sergeant Tate.

"Our mission is to scout around a section of the New Acquisitions District, northeast of here in York County. We'll gather any intelligence about the positions of armed Tories and be back in camp by sundown," Tate said. "Boots and saddles, men. We leave immediately." Of course almost no one except our commanders owned a pair of boots. We were fortunate to own a pair of shoes. It was just an army expression, I concluded.

We'd been riding our horses down a dusty road for about an hour when Bobo fell behind. I dropped back a little.

"What's the problem?"

"It's this darn mare they assigned to me since my horse is lamed up. She's too busy trying to eat weeds and plants to keep up."

I was grateful ole Dot didn't pull such shenanigans and I patted her on the neck. "Jerk her bit harder the next time she grabs something or twist her ear. Show her who's boss."

"Too bad it wasn't this horse that didn't know the password when you were on picket duty."

About that time Tate threw up his hand for us to halt.

"Three men coming our way." Sergeant Tate said. "Quick now, half of you ride into the woods on this side of the road. The rest of you come with me over here. Stay back and wait for my move."

We did as he said. I was happy the thick trees and brush offered a fine place to hide. My heart began to pound and I hoped no one could hear it. If they could, they'd know how scared I was. 'Course it was exciting at the same time. It felt sort of like hunting a bear. You never knew if you'd get him or he'd get you.

As the men rode closer, my pulse increased and my throat dried up. We didn't know if they were Tories or Whigs. At Tate's shout, we burst from the woods and surrounded the strangers.

Two of them drew their pistols with astonishing speed and fired at us. They had recognized someone in our group as a Partisan. Tate quickly fired his pistol and knocked the first shooter clean from his horse. Their first bullet hit Bobo. His body jerked back, but he stayed in his saddle. The second one missed us entirely. Three others of our squad fired their pistols at the remaining two men who tried to ride away. They both fell from their horses.

I'd not fired because I carried my rifle and couldn't very well shoot a long rifle from a horse. Thick powder smoke burned my eyes, but I saw some of our more seasoned men jump off their horses and point their pistols at the fallen men. It all happened so fast, there wasn't time to be scared. I liked the excitement for sure. I jumped off my horse and ran over to Bobo. He held the top of his left shoulder where the bullet had grazed him. He said he'd be fine.

Two of the men were dead, but one still lived.

"They're Tories all right." Sergeant Tate squatted down on one knee, cocked his second pistol, and pressed the muzzle against the wounded man's temple. "Stranger, you have one choice to make and you'll have five seconds to make it. Do you want to live or die?

He propped himself up on one elbow. "I'd prefer to live … I'll tell you anything you want to know." He wheezed because he'd been shot through a lung. He coughed up some bright red, foamy blood.

"Start crowing then. Where were you going?" "We were headed to Captain Stallions' home." "What were you going there for?"

"We were … were going to join our unit to begin making raids on Whig farms." The man coughed up more blood and turned an ashen color.

We lifted the wounded man onto his horse and brought him with us as we rode back to camp with the news. Along the way, the Tory fell off his horse and lay stone-cold dead in the middle of the road. I felt no pity for him, thinking about how his friends might attack my mother, sisters, and little Andrew. Just last week, they'd burned one neighbor's barn and threatened to kill his wife and children as they stole all the meat in their smoke house. We dragged his body to the edge of the road for his family or friends to find.

Those three Tories were the first dead men, besides John, that I'd seen so far in the war. I felt little mercy for them. It might have been one of them that killed John. I also resolved to keep an eye out for a Tory pistol, since I witnessed how useful they could be in a close fight.

Bobo wasn't hurt badly and was right proud of his wound. "Look at this, Thomas." He pulled his hunting shirt down over his shoulder to reveal where the bullet grazed him. "He pretty near got you good, Bobo," I said. "Yeah. And it stings too."

"Kennedy, put a little bear grease on Bobo's shoulder so he'll quit whining," Sergeant Tate said. "Lay that man's hat over his face and let's go. We need to get back to camp fast as we can."

"Now you've got something to impress the girls with," I said. "Don't think I haven't thought of that already."

Within ten minutes of our return, Colonel Brandon asked for forty volunteers to ride with him to capture the Tories at Stallions' place. I volunteered at once. This would be my first real engagement and it dawned on me that I could get shot and killed, just like John. Bobo came within inches of dying himself. Bullets have no conscience, I reasoned. They would kill us sixteen-year-olds just as they would kill older men. It was a chilling thought.

Captain William Love asked to be second in command with Colonel Brandon, citing the fact that his sister was Stallions' wife and he wanted to keep her safe if possible. Colonel Brandon agreed to his request.

Then Colonel Brandon talked with my messmates and me for a few minutes and gave us a small cotton bag of molasses cookies. Christopher, Bobo, William, and I munched on them like starving men.

"That'll likely be your dinner today, men. Mary Dillard baked them just this morning and sends them with her good wishes."

"Mrs. Dillard is here?" asked Bobo.

"She sure is. She accompanies Captain Dillard in camp and she's a good person to have around."

"Don't that beat all," Bobo said. "The prettiest woman in the whole district is right here in camp with us."

"We'll have to look her up and thank her." I said. We were always sneaking peeks at her during Sunday services. We concluded it wasn't sinful since God gave her such good looks in the first place.

"I'm sure she would like to see you sometime," Colonel Brandon said. "But for now, you'd best keep your minds on the Tories you'll soon be after."

I loved the cookies and the fact people like Uncle Thomas and Mary Dillard remembered us with such kindness. Except for scratching bug bites all the time and missing my mother's cooking, I was beginning to feel right at home in the militia.

William, Bobo, and I borrowed fresh horses and rode over to a meadow next to the road where the rest of the volunteers waited to ride for Stallions' place. William's father, old Squire Kennedy, accompanied us. He often got fired up when talking about how the bloody British had no right taxing us Americans without giving us political representation. "They delighted in persecuting the Scots and us Irish in the old country and now they're doing it over here." He flailed his long arms when he talked and it reminded me of a picture of a monkey we had in a book back home. We laughed at him and it sort of took the edge off things.

Christopher rode up and joined us. His cheeks were blushed and I could tell he was as excited, yet concerned as me.

"Where's Collins?" I asked.

"He said he knew better than to tempt fate when he didn't have to and he stayed behind. Said for us to watch ourselves or we'd be earth bait."

"He's smart to be cautious," William said. "He's already been in several fights and he thinks the odds are leaning against him."

"I don't think I'll ever get that way," I said. We all dismounted and stood around killing time until the officers joined us.

"I hope we get there before they all skedaddle," Christopher said.

"I've got the same concern," I said.

"Don't be too much in a hurry," William said. "Gettin' shot's no fun. Just ask Bobo."

"Yeah, just ask me." He pulled his shirt down below his shoulder to reveal a bright red burn mark beneath the bear grease William put on it to keep it from getting inflamed.

"I hope Steedham and Cunningham are there," I said. "I'd like to get them both in my sights."

I knew them well, since they lived near us. Cunningham had always been cantankerous with his neighbors, especially when it concerned our commander, Colonel Williams.

"What made Bloody Bill so mean?" Christopher asked. "He was born mean, if you ask me," said Bobo.

"John and my father and I saw Cunningham start a fist fight once with Colonel Williams," I said. "We attended a political rally when Cunningham campaigned against Colonel Williams for a seat in the South Carolina Provincial Assembly. At first, they debated calmly, but Colonel Williams lost his temper and slugged his opponent. Cunningham, being much larger than Colonel Williams, won the fight and the election. Bloody Bill viewed Colonel Williams as a mortal enemy after that ruckus and began feuding with Williams and his friends especially after the Colonel beat Cunningham in the next election. Seems like Bloody Bill has been fighting against his neighbors ever since."

"And tell them about the flogging, Thomas," Bobo said.

"Oh yes. You might not know this, but Cunningham and Steedham originally joined up with us Whigs. Then Cunningham and his bully brother began fighting with anyone whose looks they didn't like. The officers flogged them for beating up on people. Eventually, Captain William Richie, a Continental officer, turned the tables on

Bloody Bill's brother and beat him to death. After that, Bloody Bill went over to join the Tories. Steedham also left our militia and became a cowardly fence-sitter. Said he was neither a Tory nor a Whig."

"Bull manure," Bobo said.

"Steedham's worse than Cunningham," I continued. "He's even as bad as Benedict Arnold. He'd been a friend and a neighbor to all of those whom he betrayed. It might have been Bloody Bill's bullet that killed my brother, but it was Steedham's tongue that betrayed him."

Colonel Brandon rode up and addressed the patrol unit. "Gentlemen, good things don't come to those who sit around and wait. Let's be off."

We rode by twos up an old Cherokee path and toward Stallions' plantation on the upper waters of Fishing Creek near the Catawba River. It made me feel important riding after the Tories. When we got within half a mile of the place the officers ordered us to halt and close up ranks.

"Okay, men. From here on out, we must keep quiet. No talking," Colonel Brandon said. "Captain Love, you take the first twenty men and approach the house from here. Wait for the rest of us to ride around back of the house, then we'll approach in unison on foot. Captain Love will try to get his brother-in-law to surrender. If he won't we'll open up on them. But don't shoot any women or children unless they're shooting at you."

My pals and I were in Captain Love's group.

At the appointed time, we rode our horses at a slow walk toward the Stallions' house. As we got within five-hundred yards or so, we dismounted, tied our horses to a fence rail, and approached the front of the white clapboard house on foot. In this way, we could aim better and keep our horses safe at the same time. We all checked our pans to be sure the powder hadn't fallen out and re-lowered our frizzens to help keep it there.

Thinking about approaching the enemy in the open scared me plenty, but I'd force myself to remember John. Then my vengefulness drove most of the fear from my mind. Also, I didn't want to disgrace our family name by being cowardly or acting like a school boy. Still, I had to admit to myself that if it weren't for the fact that my friends were out there with me, I would just as soon pass on the experience. What's wrong with attacking from behind a barn or some other cover, I wondered.

However, I had high confidence in my .54 caliber rifle and my ability to shoot it. I'd been shooting deer with it since I turned eleven. It was much more accurate and could shoot farther than the old smooth bore muskets that the British army and many of the Tory militia carried.

"Keep moving, men. Dress up the line and be ready for anything," Captain Love softly advised. Right then I understood why they taught us the basics of foot marching. It isn't easy to keep a straight line while walking through brush and high weeds. A light wind came out of the west, but we hardly noticed.

"That's fine, men. Stay alert now," the captain said.

"Captain, there's a man over by the barn. Should some of us peel off after him?" Squire Kennedy asked.

"Let's chase one rabbit at a time. But keep an eye on him."

I walked in line with William, Bobo, Christopher, and Jonathan Steen, a friendly man about twenty-two-years old. Bobo clinched his teeth to where I could see his jaw muscles twitching. We walked within three-hundred yards of the house and still saw no signs of life.

"Better push those red locks under your hat, Christopher," Steen said. "No sense in making yourself a better target."

Christopher threw his hat off exposing a full head of curly red hair. "Let 'em try and hit me. I'll be too quick for them."

"There's that Irish blood showing," I said. Christopher smiled. As we approached within one-hundred yards of the white clapboard house, Bobo said, "There's a rifle barrel pointing out an upstairs window."

"I just saw a flash of sunlight from a barrel thrust out that top left window," William said.

"Lord, they're on to us." I said. Then I was embarrassed and resolved to press quietly forward like John would have done.

"You can say that again," Steen said. "There's a passel of them."

Then the silence became eerie. No one talked. All I could hear were the footsteps of our men swishing through the weeds. When would they shoot? When would we shoot? I remembered John's admonition to 'think before acting' and it got my mind off the danger we were walking into. I decided I'd shoot at the men in the top windows first since they would have the best opportunity to shoot us.

We got within fifty yards of the front porch when Mrs. Stallions threw open the door and ran out toward her brother, Captain Love. He ordered us to halt and hold the line. We could hear them plainly.

"Oh, William, please stop. Don't fire upon my home."

"I hope we don't have to, Mary. But we have your husband and his men surrounded and their only chance for safety is to surrender. You tell them that."

Mrs. Stallions immediately turned and ran back to the house, presumably to ask her husband and his men to surrender. She sprang upon the high door step and we heard shots from behind the house. Colonel Brandon and the Tories in the back of the house began firing at each other. One of the first shots hit Mrs. Stallions as she entered the front door.

The impact of the bullet threw her small body back out of the house and it lay crumpled on the front yard. Her white dress flapped a little in the breeze. Apparently a bullet smashed through the back door, flew through the hallway, and caught poor Mrs. Stallions in the chest. After the shock of that sad scene wore off, we knelt, cocked our rifles, and commenced firing at the Tories who now fired at us.

My first shot went through an upper window where I saw a muzzle flash. I don't know if it hit anyone and didn't wait to look. I poured another measure of powder down the muzzle of my barrel and rammed another patch and ball down with the ramrod. It seemed like it took a mighty long time to reload, but I know it must have been only around forty seconds. In the meantime, several Tory bullets zinged close by me. They sounded like angry hornets.

I aimed more carefully with the second shot and a gun barrel fell inside a second story window. There were so many people firing at the same time and so much gun smoke, I couldn't determine exactly what was happening. Musket fire crackled all over the place now. I saw Bobo shooting with one knee on the ground like the rest of us, but Christopher stood straight up and fired. I figured he'd be killed for sure.

I'd just rammed a bullet down my barrel when I saw two Tories aiming directly at William and me.

"Jump aside, William. They've got us in their sights!"

I jumped to the right and a bullet just missed me. William moved too slowly and a bullet knocked him to the ground. I'll never forget the noise from the impact. It sounded like a pick being swung into a mud hole. I finished reloading and shot one of the Tories. He fell over the window sill and his rifle dropped to the ground. He lay there hanging like one of Elizabeth's rag dolls. I crawled over to William.

"Where are you hit?"

"He got me through the wrist and my thigh is on fire. Pull me over there behind that old plow before they shoot me again."

I jumped up and dragged him behind the rusty plow that would offer him some protection. He'd been shot in the thigh and the wrist and blood flew everywhere. The bullet broke his wrist and it looked awful and blood flowed out of his thigh on both sides, front and back. I ripped off a piece of my shirt tail and tied it around his leg to help stop some of the bleeding.

"I never thought they could shoot well enough to hit me." He managed a grin. "It must have been a ricochet."

"I doubt that. I saw them aiming right at us."

"Guess I should've taken that promotion they offered me last month. Maybe I wouldn't have been in the front line." He lifted his arm up to slow the bleeding from his wrist and moaned a little. "Just what I get for volunteering."

"Probably wouldn't have made any difference. Fate is fate." I tied my handkerchief around his wrist to stop the bleeding.

"You go on now and give 'em what for, Thomas. I think I'll be all right."

"Yeah, you'll be fine, but you'll need a heap of mending. It's amazing what damage one bullet can do."

"Thanks for the encouragement." He smiled, but had tears of pain in his eyes.

I moved over a few yards, picked up my rifle, reloaded, and fired a couple more times. Squire Kennedy worked his way over to tend to his son. About that time I saw a man running through an open field near the barn. I raised my rifle to shoot, but someone shouted, "Don't fire. He's one of our men." I lowered my rifle and the man stopped, turned, and fired at us. Squire Kennedy quickly aimed and fired. The man dropped dead.

"That'll fix him," Kennedy said. "They shouldn't have shot my boy." Squire Kennedy was an excellent marksman. It turned out that the dead man was recognized as a partisan, but in reality, had been a spy for the Tories.

Just after this incident, a Tory thrust a white flag, tied to the end of a rifle, out a window. Someone from our side immediately shot the rifle and in a moment a new flag came out, tied to a ram rod. This seemed like a more sincere surrender and Captain Love and Colonel Brandon accepted it.

A little while later we learned they wounded several of our men, but no one died. Squire Kennedy was preparing to take William home and I wondered if we would ever see him again. He looked pale, but was awake as I walked over.

"Hey, Thomas," William called as he lay there stretched out in one of Stallions' wagons on a pile of hay. "Thanks for your help.

Don't know when I'll see you again, but I'll try to get back soon. Can't let my father fight all by himself."

"Don't worry about it. Just get well."

"I'm counting on you to take care of our messmates … especially Collins. He's a good person. Never had a family since both parents died when he was a baby. And the grandmother who raised him died last winter. We're about all the family he's got."

"Didn't know all that." I shoved my fingers through my hair. "I'll look after him and the others. Take care of yourself."

"I will. Just remember, John wouldn't want you to get yourself killed on his account. Fight hard, but don't take too many chances. And that goes for that crazy Christopher as well. You're a natural leader and we need leaders."

"Thanks. I'll keep it in mind." I shook his good hand.

"Giddy up there," the wagon driver called. The horses began pulling the creaking wagon down the lane. Squire Kennedy rode his horse ahead of it.

"Remember the cause, Thomas. You're fighting for the cause."

I watched my friend roll away out of sight before returning to the main body of our patrol. I walked over toward the barn where Captain Jolly had gathered his men.

"We killed two Tories and wounded four more," Captain Jolly said. "And we captured twenty-eight able-bodied men. Colonel Brandon sent them with a guard detail to Charlotte, North Carolina where they'll be imprisoned."

"Too bad that's all we got," Christopher said.

Captain Love and Captain Stallions held a tearful reunion. Captain Stallions said his fighting days were over and Colonel Brandon gave him a parole to bury his wife and get his affairs in order. He would have to leave the district.

We were all proud we struck such a crushing blow to the Tories, but I was disappointed I found neither Steedham nor Cunningham there. Bobo, Christopher, and Steen and I walked back to our horses and sat around waiting for the officers to lead us back to our home camp.

"You'll get Cunningham and Steedham another time, Thomas," Bobo said. "I'll bet money on it."

"I hope you're right."

"You'd best hope you find them soon," Steen said. "The way those balls came at us today, it's hard to tell how many more battles any of us will survive. The odds of getting killed increase with each fight you know. That's why you don't see many veterans volunteering to get in harm's way." He held up his black slouch hat and poked his finger through a bullet hole. This impressed us all very much and Steen became our hero for having escaped sudden death by a half-inch. Just thinking about Steen's close call caused old man fear to creep back into my head. I realized that I could have easily been wounded like William or even killed. This fighting wasn't child's play, but it was exhilarating. Little did I know then how wrong I was to think it was fun.

INTO THE FRAY

July 1780

After the fight at Stallions', things got pretty quiet in our part of South Carolina, but we heard about several fights outside our district. Most notably the Partisans, under General Sumter, won a key battle against the Tories at Ramseur's Mill in North Carolina toward the end of June. Colonel Williams' and Colonel Brandon's regiments camped together and gave several companies extended furlough. Those in my company got to go home. This was a bittersweet moment for me. I loved being in the field with the militia and I could hardly wait for an opportunity to get even with those who killed John. Nevertheless, going home to Mother's cooking and being with the family held great appeal. My father's company volunteered to stay active in the camp while the rest of us left the field.

You'd have thought the prodigal son came home that afternoon in mid-July when I rode into the yard. Jane and Elizabeth were making soap in a big tub near the kitchen house. Red commenced to barking and Elizabeth screamed something about my being home. Everyone came out to greet me. Mother and Andrew came from the house and Hank and two field hands came from the barn.

"Thomas is home. Thomas is home. Hello, Thomas." Andrew yelled as he ran ahead of everyone. I slid off my horse, caught Andrew as he jumped into my arms, and swung him around like I always did. He squealed with delight.

"Thomas, you look older," Elizabeth said. "Ah, that's just because he's dirty," Jane said.

Andrew shouted, "He's not dirty, he's my big brother and don't be picking on him so fast. He just got here."

"Thanks. It's nice to know someone defends me." I lowered him to the ground and led Dot over to a hitching post near the barn. Andrew followed me, patting Dot's shoulder.

"Did you get shot or anything, Thomas?"

"No, Andrew, but I got shot at and I gave them back more than they sent."

"Where did that happen?" Elizabeth asked.

"At the Stallions' Plantation up in the New Acquisition District over near the Catawba River. I'll tell you all about it later." My mother walked over to me.

"Hello, Mother."

"Let me see you, Thomas." She held me with her arms stretched out looking at me. "Just turn around and let me see that you're all right."

"I'm fine and I can't wait to get some of your home cooking." "You'll get plenty of that real soon. We're baking some chickens right now … that reminds me, Andrew Paul, go on over to the garden and pull me a peck of chard like I asked you an hour ago. Then go down to the root cellar and fetch me ten good sized potatoes." Mother gave Andrew that stern look we all knew so well and he walked off muttering to himself, "And why are you so filthy, Thomas? Haven't you taken a bath at all?"

"Ha, ha, Elizabeth," Jane said. "Mother thinks he's dirty too." "Guess I am a little soiled. I did wash up in the Broad River some time back though. Thanks, girls, for making up all that soap for me. I'll get to it as soon as I say hello to Hank and them." They were standing there waiting their turn. I greeted them all and it was a joy to see these men whom I'd worked with since I was about eight years old.

"Hey, Thomas, good to have you back. Now maybe we can make some progress around here," Hank said. "With everybody gone, they's hardly enough of us to get it all done." I shook his hand and thanked him and the others for their hard work and for looking after Mother and the children. These were free men, but they earned their keep by working for my father. Our place was too big for us to work alone and we were mighty happy to have the help. Hank told me Mother had given him my father's old fowling gun to carry around since the Tory hostilities had been increasing lately. It wasn't much good at long range, but it was deadly at close range. I began to loosen Dot's saddle, but Hank and his hands insisted on doing that chore for me.

"Let us do that. You go on and rest up. We'll curry ole Dot and grain her," Hank said as he grabbed the reigns and headed toward the barn.

"Thomas, what news do you have of your father?" Mother asked.

"He's just fine. He volunteered to keep his company in the camp until those of us on furlough return. Then he'll be home. Here's a letter he sent you and he told me to kiss you and the children for him." I gave her the letter and leaned over and kissed Mother on the cheek. I then pretended to kiss Jane and Elizabeth, but they jumped away just as sisters do about such things.

"How long is your furlough?"

"Two weeks, unless they call us back sooner."

"That should be time enough to get the dirt off you, get you a new set of clothes, and feed you proper." Mother jerked my shirt collar and said, "Let's go to the house and you can get ready for a hot bath … then I can wash and mend these rags you've been wearing."

After enjoying a fine chicken dinner, Andrew and I sat in sapling chairs on our front porch and watched the golden sun drift below the fields. Father and John and I had built those chairs just last winter. Our place was on the east side of the road near Brown's Creek northeast of the Duncan Presbyterian meeting house. Hardwood trees, mostly oak and hickory, stood on the ridges of the rolling hills and along the creek. Those woods had deer, wolves, wild boars, and cougars. The flat areas were filled with pine trees and a few good open meadows, but we cleared about another thirty acres for planting corn, wheat, and barley, that we could eat or have ground at Williams' mill to sell to others. Father always said the sandy soil was just right for growing things.

Like everyone else, we raised about everything we ate or needed for making our clothes. In the garden we raised sweet corn, beans, squash, and okra by the bushel. Keeping the raccoons, deer, and other critters out of there was the dog's responsibility. Mother and the girls kept up with the house and garden, spun cotton and flax thread, made soap, cooked, and sang songs or held devotionals in the evenings. Father and we boys and three field hands worked the fields, tended the livestock, built fences for the cows and horses, and we fished and hunted once in a while. Hank was the lead field hand and managed when Father was away. He and his small family lived on our place about a quarter mile down the road toward Hammond's store.

After about a half a day's rest and four or five day's work in the hot July sun, Barrum Bobo came for a visit and gave us an excuse to stop working and rest for part of an afternoon. He told us about a battle over at Brattonsville, northeast of us between the Broad and Catawba Rivers in York County.

"It happened on the same day we fought at Stallions' plantation. My father drove a wagon through the country west of Charlotte, North Carolina and south along the Catawba River just after the battle," Bobo began. "He went over to the Hill foundry to see if there were any swords left after the British regulars attacked the Partisans there last month. Almost nothing remained and the ironworks was closed down. Some neighbors told my father the proprietor, Billy Hill, joined the Partisans with Colonel William Bratton to fight back. Father says it was a terrible blow to us 'cause the foundry produced about all the munitions and farming implements for the upstate country."

We all sat on the front porch in the shade drinking fresh tea cooled at the well house. We loved it when people visited, especially if they brought any news we hadn't heard. Jane wore a dress and sat close to Bobo.

"How's your tea, Barrum?" she asked with a smile.

"It's about the best tea I ever drank," he smiled. We seldom get any at the camp. Did you make it?"

"Of course. I make all the tea here. Mama says tea's the house wine of the South and I make it the best."

"I couldn't agree more with your mother."

"Thank you, Barrum." Jane laid her hand on Bobo's arm. "One secret is to put the sugar in the tea water before you boil it."

"Okay, Jane. Your tea is delicious and we all love it," I said. "Could we get back to Bobo's story?" She withdrew her hand slowly and Bobo blushed. I never saw her act so coy before this.

He took another drink of tea and began again. "It was that same Captain Huck who raided the Hill Iron works. Father says Huck was a marauding provincial who came down here from Philadelphia and joined Tarleton's dragoons. He and about 150 Dragoons and Tories surrounded Colonel Bratton's house seeking to capture him, since he's one of Colonel Sumter's key officers. Mrs. Bratton told Huck her husband wasn't home. They threatened to cut off her head with a reaping knife, but she held her ground. Huck and his men left in disgust and rode over to the next plantation, Williamson's I think it was, and camped for the night." Bobo stopped, swigged some tea, and smiled at Jane. Jane smiled and Elizabeth snickered.

"What happened next?" Andrew asked. "Please go on, Barrum," Jane said.

"A servant named Watt sneaked off and told Colonel Bratton what happened and where Huck and his men were camped. Just before daylight Bratton and his four-hundred South Carolina Militia attacked Huck's camp and caught them by surprise. The battle ended quickly and Huck was killed, shot through the back of the head as he tried to escape. Father says it was an important victory since the Partisans defeated British-trained Provincials as well as the Tories."

"I'm just sorry we weren't part of it," I said. "Were Cunningham or Steedham involved?"

"I don't know the particulars of who all was involved except those

I mentioned."

"How many were killed?" asked Andrew.

"He said forty were killed, many wounded, and most of the rest of them were captured. Father said he heard only one of the Whigs died."

"Sounds like a mighty fine piece of work, if you ask me," Jane said.

"Amen to that, Jane," Mother said. "But I hate it that men must die and mothers like me have to grieve over their dead." She wiped tears away with her handkerchief. Upon hearing this story bout Huck's defeat, I could hardly wait to get back to soldiering. Bobo returned to his home later that afternoon. He didn't dare ride home in the dark with all the Tories roaming about.

When church services were over that next Sunday, Bobo and I left to return to camp. He kicked a bench outside the church as he told me how some Tories threw rocks into their well. "Those witlings did a good job of it. My father and I worked two days to clean it out." It seemed like we heard about new atrocities from the Tories every day. He also asked a lot of questions about Jane. I think he was going sweet on her. It sort of made me jealous, in a way. He had a girl interested in him, even if it was my sister. And I didn't think any girls even gave me a second thought, especially after that Patsy Lynch disaster.

After arriving back at our regimental camp, I visited with my father before he went home on furlough.

"Nothing exciting happened while you were gone," Father said, "but we heard Major William Davie, a cavalry officer under General Sumter, whipped the enemy at a place called Hanging Rock over east of the Catawba River. And some of General Sumter's men initiated a battle at the British garrison near Rocky Mount, South Carolina. They set the building on fire, but a sudden thunderstorm put it out and Sumter withdrew."

"Too bad about that. Did you hear about Huck's defeat at Brattonsville?"

"Yes. Mr. Bobo came through here a few days ago to deliver some provisions and he told us. Things are heating up again. General Cornwallis and his British troops are moving deeper into the backcountry and establishing garrisons all over the place and he's established a new command headquarters at Camden. That's a hundred miles inland from Charleston. South Carolina's Governor Rutledge and some of his advisors have moved to North Carolina to keep from being captured by Cornwallis." He leaned over and pulled a sweet weed out of its stem and began to chew on it for the sweetness. I did the same. Then he hugged me and patted me on the back. "Stay alert and be smart, Thomas. Make your Uncle and me proud of you." He mounted his horse to leave. "And don't forget the good book, son. Mathew chapter seven has some good advice. Verse seven is particularly encouraging. See you in a couple of weeks if not before." He gently heeled his horse and rode off in a trot toward home.

"Matthew seven, seven," I repeated so I wouldn't forget. I knew my father and knew he'd ask about it when he next saw me. Father wanted all of his children to stay close to the Lord and that's why he tried to keep us reading the Bible. I didn't mind studying the Bible on Sundays, but often found it difficult to read every night especially when tired from working in the fields all day. I liked to read how God Almighty helped the Israelites win all their battles as long as they did what God wanted. I hoped we Partisans were doing what God wanted so he'd be on our side.

After reporting for duty and settling in, Bobo and I decided to walk over the whole camp and visit folks. The drilling didn't start until morning and we had plenty of free time. In fact, camp life could get pretty boring. If we weren't training or preparing and eating meals, we looked for something to occupy our time. My favorite past-times were racing horses, playing cards, and fishing.

This afternoon, we walked to the headquarters area and looked around. Horses and supply wagons stretched down the road a long way. Bobo and I wondered about all the food and camping accouterments they carried. Our appreciation for the quartermasters increased. Keeping an army supplied with food and utensils and ammunition was no small feat.

"What do you think of all these provisions men?" asked a man behind us. We turned and there stood Colonel Williams. We came to attention and threw up a salute at once. He returned the salute and smiled. He was an impressive looking man. I'd never seen a general, but if I ever did, I expected he'd look like Colonel Williams.

"It takes a lot of work to keep this regiment supplied. Fortunately, General Sumter recently shared some of the stores he commandeered at Ramseur's Mill," the Colonel said. "Most new recruits think wars are won by those who have the most men and the best marksmen. But wars are really won by which army is best fed and best equipped. And you young men require a considerable amount of food." He chuckled, spread out his arms, and slapped us both on our shoulders. We liked Colonel Williams and his whole family.

"Daniel, Joseph," he called to his sons. "Come on out and say hello to Mr. Young and Mr. Bobo."

Daniel and Joseph walked out of their tent. "Hello, Thomas. Hey there, Barrum," greeted Daniel. Daniel was a member of our Sunday school class, but Joseph, who was only ten years old, was in the younger group. They were sworn members of the militia just like us. We visited for over an hour and talked about everything from fighting to fishing, both of which we hoped to be doing soon.

"Don't forget to come and see us over in Carlisle Company," I said as we rose to leave.

"We'll come over real soon, but don't leave just yet," Daniel said. "Mrs. Dillard will be put out if she knew you came by and didn't pay your respects."

"Mrs. Dillard is camped here?" asked Bobo.

"She sure is," Joseph replied. "She and Captain Dillard stay in that tent just yonder."

"Let's go see her," I suggested. All of us boys stayed enamored with the young Mrs. Dillard, even if she was married.

Sure enough, Mary Ramage Dillard was there setting a Dutch oven in the coals of her fire when we walked up. "Boys, boys, boys! It's so good to see you." Her face was angelic and without a single wrinkle. To our delight, she hugged both Bobo and me. Her silky black hair smelled like heaven.

"Sit down and let's find out all about you and your families. If you can stay for a few minutes, I'll share this blackberry cobbler I'm baking for James and a new boy in camp named Joe Kerr." She lifted some coals and set them on the lid of the Dutch oven. "You'll like Joe. He's about sixteen and hails from Mecklenburg County in North Carolina. He can't speak much at all, but he hears just fine and he loves the cause." We waited for that cobbler with much anticipation and tried not to stare at Mary's pretty face or her femininity too much. Her dark eyes and perpetual smile brought joy to everyone.

"If your cobbler is anywhere nearly as good as those molasses cookies, it will be wonderful," Bobo said. This pleased Mary and she hugged him for it. I wished I had thought to thank her for those cookies before he did.

Fifteen minutes later, Captain Dillard and Joe came up and after the introductions, we ate Mrs. Dillard's cobbler. We all swore it was the best blackberry cobbler ever made. That's one benefit about eating out in the open. Everything did taste better. 'Course we asked all about how she made the cobbler so we could do the same at our mess.

Joe Kerr was a skinny boy who walked with a limp, had a shriveled arm, and looked like he was daft. He couldn't talk clearly because the roof of his mouth was all misshaped, but he drew pictures and words on the bare ground with a stick and sometimes he used pencil and paper. Mary explained that he left his Tory parents who lived near Charlotte and found a Whig outfit under Colonel McDowell that took him in. Later, the Dillards sort of adopted him and he joined our regiment. He already proved to be a valuable asset.

"Joe walks right into those Tory camps and comes out well fed and full of information," Mary said. "Isn't that right, Joe?" Joe nodded. "They don't pay him any attention since he's no obvious threat and he pretends not to have enough sense to draw water from a well." She brushed his dark hair out of his eyes with her hand and he blushed. "But he's plenty smart enough and he's become one of the best spies in the South."

After finishing the cobbler, Captain Dillard pulled out his fiddle and played some lively tunes like *The Sow Had the Measles* and *We'll Go Froggin' Tonight*. Then he played *The Girl I Left Behind* very slowly and softly while Mary Dillard sang the words. She sang with a clear and warm voice. We finished the singing with *All Hail the Power of Jesus' Name* and *Amazing Grace,* a fairly new song which we sang most every Sunday at the meeting house. It was a beautiful and memorable evening.

Bobo and I walked to our tent in the dark, but there were plenty of camp fires to light the way.

"What part of tonight did you like the best?" Bobo asked.

"It's a toss-up between the cobbler and the singing. I especially liked hearing Mary's voice," I said.

"I especially enjoyed watching her move. The way her hips sway when she walks is enough to set me to dreaming," Bobo said.

"You better not let Captain Dillard hear you talking like that.

He'll thump your noggin for talking that way."

"Oh, don't be so straight laced. She's beautiful to behold and I saw you doing your share of looking too." He was right about that and I had to admit that I hoped to have a wife just like her someday. That is if I ever mange to find a girl that cottons to me and if I can get up the nerve to even speak to her without embarrassing myself.

Two weeks later near the middle of August, word spread throughout the camp that the British regulars along with their Tory friends were moving into our district to rout us out. One of our reconnaissance patrols saw a large group of the enemy moving toward Musgrove's Mill down on the Enoree River. Colonel Williams called for pickets to be posted at a mile perimeter around camp and he and his key officers, including Uncle Thomas and my father, who returned to camp about two weeks back, met for most of the morning.

To make matters worse, we received news General Horatio Gates, the hero of the battle of Saratoga, had been completely defeated as he launched a surprise attack at Camden. Lord Cornwallis and his British Regulars scared off the partisan militia and practically annihilated the Continentals. General Gates high-tailed it back up to North Carolina leaving his remaining troops to fend for themselves. This meant there were practically no trained Continental troops in the Carolinas and we militia were the only resistance against the largest and most feared army in the world. And as if this news wasn't bad enough, General Sumter and his militia troops were ambushed on Fishing Creek by Banister Tarleton and soundly defeated. Sumter barely escaped in his underclothes. Now that would be a sight to see, I thought.

I'd never seen a British Regular, but I could imagine how intimidating they were in their bright red uniforms. I saw a picture of their honor guards once in a book. Those elite grenadier infantry guards with their tall black bearskin hats were most imposing.

"Captain Jolly said the green-coated dragoons are the most frightful," I said during an evening mess, "since they ride tall horses and are excellent swordsmen."

"It don't matter at all what those British are wearing," Bobo said. "They'll bleed just like the rest of us. Besides, those red coats will make easy marks to shoot at." He scooped up some beans with a piece of cornbread. "Up north along the coast, the patriots call them lobsterbacks because of those red coats."

"Lobsterbacks, or Bloodybacks, what's the difference?" Collins said. "This next fight won't be as easy as you boys had it at Stallions' Plantation."

"Course it will," Bobo said. "But if you're afraid to run with the big dogs, you should stay on the porch like last time."

"Humph! Fighting those Tories at Stallions' plantation was like a quilting bee compared with what we're facing now. When you see those British Regulars and their dragoons coming for you, you'll likely pee your pants and run for home."

"That'll be a cold day in hell, Collins," I blurted. "If you're so scared, just stay behind me and Bobo. We'll protect you." I surprised myself for challenging an older man and a veteran. But just being older and more experienced doesn't make a man right, I reasoned.

"Ha! The day I need two greenhorns to protect me is the day I leave this militia outfit." He stood up to emphasize his height over us. "But I would like to see how you stand up to some real fightin' so stick close when it all begins." He smiled, "Hope you shoot the British as well as you shoot horses, Thomas."

Christopher turned from the Dutch oven he was tending, his face turning red, and he jumped up clenching his fists. "You want me to knock his teeth out, Thomas?"

"No, Christopher. Don't let him goad you into anything stupid. Fighting will just get you lashes." I stood up and faced Collins. "Guess you can't help being so insulting since it's in your nature, but pay close attention when the fighting starts. You'll see some straight shooting," I said. "But right now, why don't we check on our peach cobbler so we can dwell on the positive for a while. It smells mighty good." This suggestion calmed Christopher down.

"It's bound to be good," Christopher said. "After all, I fixed it just like Mary Dillard told us.

Collins relaxed and said he was sorry for being so sharp tongued. I figured he was just worrying about facing British Regulars so he had to boast some about his being a good fighter and all. In truth, he was talking himself into a scare.

The cobbler wasn't anything much to look at, but it tasted wonderful. We had 'commandeered' the Dutch oven from the commissary wagon one dark night and it became our most valuable cooking accoutrement.

By the next morning, we learned Joe Kerr, who some called Mary Dillard's boy, had wandered casually into the British camp on the Enoree River at Musgrove's Mill about forty miles from our position. He arrived back at our camp early that morning and reported the positions of their units and said more than three-hundred men camped there. We had only about half that number.

After a quick breakfast of some hard boiled eggs and barley mush, Captain Jolly ordered our company to pack up a full day's food rations and prepare enough bullets for a major fight. Bobo and Christopher and I melted about a pound of lead apiece which produced about thirty balls. Then we waited and waited some more. At dusk, we mounted up and moved out toward Musgrove's Mill. Evidently Colonel Williams didn't want any British spies to observe our movements.

Along the way, additional militia units commanded by Colonels Shelby and Clarke joined us. These additional troops gave us more confidence that we could whip the British in a fair fight.

We rode nearly all night and rested our horses at Horseshoe Falls on Cedar Shoals Creek. We set up a fireless camp there just a mile or so from the Enoree River and Musgrove's Mill. The officers ordered us to keep our saddles on the horses and to speak softly.

Christopher whispered, "If anything happens to me, I want you to tell my father that I died facing the enemy."

"Just don't do any fool thing and nothing will happen," I said. "Besides, everybody, including your father, knows you'll always face the enemy." I don't mind saying we were all getting a little squeamish about fighting the regulars.

Thirty minutes later Captain Jolly addressed us. "Men, we'll be deploying on a hillside north of the Enoree River near the mill where the British are camped. Tie up anything that makes noise and walk your horses. After we get into position, we'll tether our horses about fifty yards over the hill top. Then we'll come back down the hill and fortify our positions. Use trees, brush, or anything else that provides some protection. We've got about an hour until sunrise. And mind your rifles carefully. Keep them empty and pointed away from others and yourself until told to load up. We lost a man from Colonel William's regiment yesterday who accidentally shot himself while leaning on his barrel."

This news sent chills up my spine. I'd leaned on my rifle hundreds of times and never thought about the risk of being shot. I could easily imagine what damage could be done to a person's body at such close range.

Forty minutes later we positioned ourselves behind the brush we'd piled up. We were told to load our rifles. As the British awoke, we saw them start their breakfast fires. They were camped all over a field that paralleled the river.

"Would you look at that," whispered Bobo. "They're sure enough down there and it looks like there's a passel of 'em."

"You better dig a hole and get in it, boys," Collins said. "It's gonna get hot pretty quick now."

"Where'd you learn to whisper, Collins? In a sawmill?" Bobo asked.

"Hush up!" commanded Sergeant Tate. "No talking. We'll be baiting them up here any minute now. And stay out of sight until ordered to fire."

You could cut the tension with a knife as we sat there in silence loading our rifles. I glanced behind me to be sure there was an escape route in case we needed one. "Buck up," I reminded myself. "You're replacing John now so don't shame him."

"And don't forget to pick your touch holes, add fresh prime, and be ready to shoot when told," Tate added.

We'd already primed our pans, dropped our frizzens, and loaded our rifles, but we double checked them nonetheless.

Five minutes ticked by, then I saw about twenty-five of our Partisans ride to within fifty yards of the British camp and fire at them from just across the river at the ford. The British scrambled in confusion for only a moment, then they returned fire. This skirmish went on for a few minutes and I saw men fall on both sides. Without warning a group of dragoons came charging across the river at our men who turned and rode straight up the hill toward us. The British drummers drummed out the call to action.

"Here they come," Collins said.

"Not quite yet," I said. "The dragoons have held up."

"They're waiting for the infantry to get in position," Bobo said.

"Looks like they've taken the bait." Christopher said. He took his hat off and threw it down as he stared at the scene below. "That'll give them something to aim at," he said as he tousled his shaggy red hair.

Sure enough we saw company after company of British Provincials in red coats cross the ford, line up, and begin marching toward us. The original Partisan attackers tied up their horses with ours and joined us for the battle. It was a beautiful sight to see. The red uniforms and white and blue flags appeared to float across the ground and up the hill.

"Prepare to fire," Sergeant Tate said.

Bobo clenched his teeth and Christopher sat bare headed, eyes forward.

The enemy closed to within fifty yards of us and Captain Jolly shouted, "Take them, men!" We fired our first volley directly into their front line. Gun smoke swirled thickly in the air, but we clearly saw many British soldiers fall and others stumble out of line. Still, the next rank kept coming. I loaded my rifle as fast as I could and so did my friends. "Fire at will. Fire low, fire low," our officers shouted.

Christopher stood up to fire, oblivious to the danger. "Kneel down," Tate said. "They'll kill you for sure.

"Don't worry about him, Sarge," Collins shouted. "He's so short he don't even have to duck."

"I'm not afraid of them," Christopher said as he knelt down and fired. "And shut up about my height, you crooked-nosed bean pole."

John wouldn't expose himself like that, I thought. He once told me, "Shooting men was a lot like squirrel hunting. You have to outsmart them. You have to get a bead on them before they see you. Just sit still and wait for opportunities."

I just finished ramming a ball down my barrel when the provincials unleashed their first volley. Balls hit brush and trees, but very few of our men. I looked for an opportunity to find a clear target and fired at an officer on a horse. He slumped over and rode out of the line of fire. The British prepared to charge us with bayonets. I could see the flash of their cold steel knives at the end of their musket barrels. The hair on the back of my neck stood up. "God help us," I said out loud to myself.

"Here they come. Get ready," Captain Jolly shouted.

We knew we would be killed if they got to us with those bayonets because we didn't have any and our rifles weren't equipped to hold them if we did. I fired at the red wall, but it kept coming unfazed. We fired again and again and the bayonet charge finally stalled. They were too exposed to our withering fire to continue up the hill. Slowly, they fell back across the river. The officers ordered us to follow them a short distance and keep firing. Christopher jumped out first and tripped, but got back up and led the way. We followed him, but this action lasted only a few minutes before all the British forded the shallow river and we were ordered back to our original position.

The open hillside was strewn with dead and wounded British soldiers. At least half of their force lay on that hill and the other half retreated from the battle. We'd won! We met the British for the first time and whipped them. A loud shout went up from our side. "Huzzah! Huzzah!" We yelled until we grew hoarse. Some of us threw our hats in the air.

"Nice job, boys," Collins said after things quieted down and we walked up the hill to retrieve our horses. "I'm pleased you didn't shame yourselves by running away."

"Ha!" Bobo said. "I was taking bets you'd be the one to skedaddle. And you cost me three shillings." He glanced at me and winked.

"Serves you right for disrespecting your elder. Too bad they didn't bilk you for more than that."

Collins fought hard, I'll give him that, but he'd belittle you in a heartbeat. I figured he did that just to build up his confidence.

We lost only four men and had seven wounded while the British had over 150 soldiers killed or wounded. Among my friends, only Christopher was wounded. In his haste to chase the retreating British, he fell on a sharp rock and cut his arm.

"Look at this," Christopher showed us a three-inch gash on his forearm. "Now, maybe I've got something to show the girls."

"If you weren't in such an all-fired hurry to prove how brave you are, you wouldn't have hurt yourself," Bobo said. "Besides, it's not the same as if you were shot or stabbed."

"Aw, it's nothing but a scratch anyway," Collins said. "Just remember, you don't have to be brave to prove how stupid you are. Quit taking all those chances."

I cut off Christopher's shirt tail and wrapped it around his forearm. "Better get that looked at soon as you can before it festers," I told him. "Someone will probably have to sew you up."

We relished in our success, but I must admit I felt some sympathy and respect for those poor soldiers who marched directly into our fire with no protection whatsoever. Slowly, I began to understand I was fighting for liberty as much as to avenge my brother. Remembering my father's admonitions, I even took a moment to send up a silent prayer of thanks for our victory and safety.

The British commander, Colonel Innes, petitioned Colonel Williams to collect their dead and wounded. We watched as they loaded up their fallen men into wagons. The sun rose warm in the sky and we could smell the blood and gore from the dead bodies. It reminded me of hog slaughtering back home in November. John usually slit their throats. They squealed pathetically and bled all over the place.

The British then left Musgrove's Mill for Cornwallis' main camp at Camden. We returned to our base camp as did the other militia units that had joined us. My, we were proud soldiers.

Nothing of consequence happened in our district for about a month. Father and I got to go home on furlough for two weeks in September to bring in a third hay cutting. After our victory at Musgrove's Mill, the local Tories pretty much behaved themselves. Then word came that Cornwallis established a headquarters near Winnsboro, deeper into the backcountry, and was preparing to march all the way up to Charlotte. The officers reactivated us at once.

Major Patrick Ferguson, the best shot in the British army and the inventor of their best rifle, commanded a large force of British provincials and Tory militia. He was marching west again into our upstate country to quell what they called "the rebellion" in the Carolina backcountry.

Major Ferguson sent a message to our leaders. Colonels Williams and Brandon assembled the regiments to hear the message. Williams read it aloud: "If you do not desist from your opposition to British arms and take protection under my standard, I will march my army over the mountains, hang your leaders, and lay your country to waste with fire and sword."

"Hang the bugger!" Christopher said.

"We'll give him our swords if he comes out here." Collins said. We got all fired up by these threats. And we still felt our oats since we'd repelled the British at Musgrove's Mill.

Ferguson later made disparaging comments about upstate and mountain women. News of his threats reached us in quick order and they enraged every Partisan who lived in these districts and well beyond. Patriotic fever ran high.

"The fat's in the fire now," Captain Jolly told us. "Be prepared to move on a moment's notice. Ferguson will be paying us a visit soon and he'll likely outnumber us. But remember, we fight for liberty and for our women and children and they're fighting only because it's their job. That gives us an advantage."

Later that night we heard that the Patriot, Colonel Frances Marion, successfully beat the British up and down the Pee Dee River over toward the South Carolina Coast, but it gave us little comfort. Cornwallis was moving toward Charlotte and Patrick 'Bulldog' Ferguson, as some called him, would be coming for us. As we prepared to enter our leaky tents to sleep, Bobo said what was on everyone's mind. "I wonder how many of us will be alive a week from now."

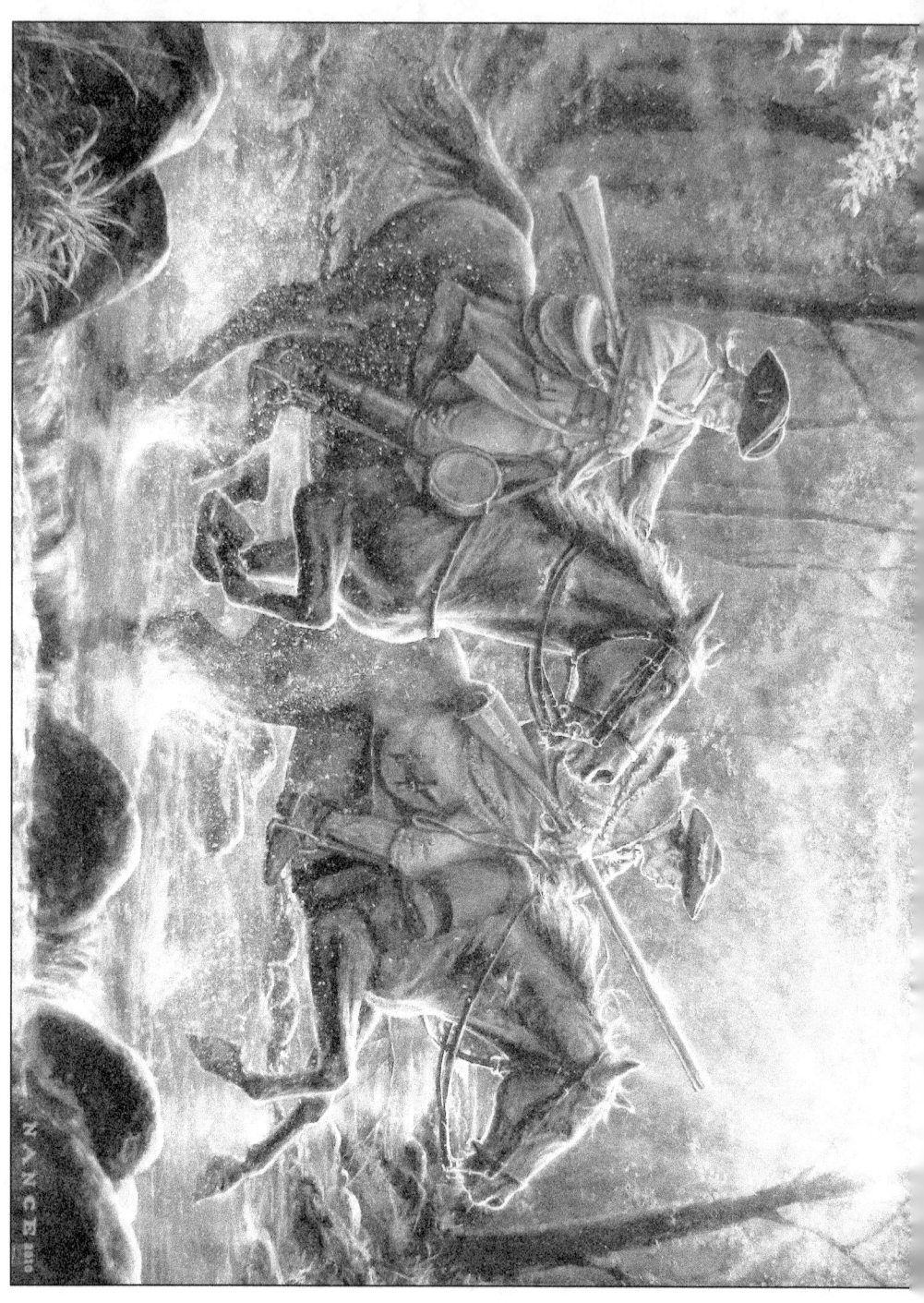

Patriots by Dan Nance

UP THE MOUNTAIN

October 1780

We knew there would likely be another imminent battle when Captain Jolly told us Major Ferguson and his troops marched into our territory yesterday. Our commanders sent couriers over the mountains to communicate Ferguson's threat and to solicit help from Partisans. The couriers went west over the mountains, into the Tennessee country, and to upper North Carolina, Georgia, and Virginia.

"Boys, you can bet we'll be in the thick of it when we take on Ferguson and his men," Collins told us. We'd just finished our evening meal and sat around the fire. "This won't be no easy fight like down there at Musgrove's Mill. You ladies will have to keep your heads low and carry your best good luck pieces to survive this one."

"Aw hush up, Collins. All you ever do is look at the negative," I told him. Bobo and Christopher agreed with me. "We conducted ourselves pretty well at Musgrove's Mill and I recall you were about as antsy as the rest of us."

Bobo chimed in. "And you were the one talking about digging a hole for protection. We whipped Ferguson once and we can do it again."

"I didn't need no hole. I just tried to protect you three from getting hurt." Collins squinted at us and held his nose high. "After all, I'm the one with the most experience around here."

"Keep flying high and you'll light in the cow dab," Christopher said.

"I ain't boasting. But I've been around longer than you boys and I've learned never to underestimate the enemy. Remember, the captain says Ferguson has twice as many men as us. Well over a thousand."

"Good. Then we can kill a whole lot more of them than we did last month," Christopher said.

"That's the spirit!" I said. "The problem with you, Collins, is you've been fighting too long and you're getting cynical."

"Okay, Young. I'll still be there to help keep you boys alive, even if you don't want to listen to me. My advice, however, is that you commence to reading your Bibles and prayin' tonight. You never know what tomorrow will bring."

Collins' words were almost prophetic. On the very next morning the officers ordered us to prepare three days rations, fill our canteens, and be ready to begin a campaign to find Ferguson and his troops before they penetrated too deeply into the backcountry.

Sergeant Tate said partisan militia were on their way from as far away as Virginia.

My father came to see me after the first day on the march. He'd taken ill and decided to go home to recuperate. Dysentery and lung problems had bothered him for about a week. I worried about his health and offered to accompany him home, but he wouldn't hear of it. He insisted he would be all right and I should stay with the regiment. Then he gave me some advice like fathers often do.

"I know you want to avenge John … all of us do. But you won't do him any good by dying yourself. Staying alive is a valuable skill, even a virtue, I think. And by staying alive, you can do more good for the cause than otherwise."

"I know. Don't worry about me. I'll keep my wits like you taught me."

"And remember that there's two kinds of liberty," he told me. "There's the political kind that we're fighting for, and the spiritual kind. He let that sort of settle in some, and then he followed it up. "Both are important freedoms and neither should be neglected. Keep reading the good book son and remember to put your faith in the Lord." At this point, I have to admit that I wasn't thinking too much about either kind of liberty. I just wanted to kill those who killed John.

I figured it would take some of my pain away … to even the score.

After praying for me and the regiment, he hugged me and rode off toward home.

Even though we didn't see each other much since we served in different companies, I always knew he was nearby. I never experienced such loneliness as I did at that moment when I watched him ride down the road and out of sight. The little boy in me rose up that evening and I began thinking about what he'd said before leaving. Later that night in the tent I even read some verses in the Bible, thinking it would please my father and it might get my mind off my loneliness. I pondered on that verse Father always quoted, "Where the spirit of Lord is there is liberty." I remember thinking that surely God favored our side. Then I fell to sleep wondering what tomorrow would bring.

We continued riding toward the Northeast for two days and arrived at the Cowpens near the North Carolina border. Local farmers penned up their cows here to fatten them up before herding them to market in area towns to sell. It was a good camp since the cows kept the grass short. The terrain lay mostly flat and open among scattered pines. We joined a sizable force of about one hundred and fifty over-the-mountain men commanded by Colonels Campbell, Shelby, McDowell, and Sevier. Colonel Cleveland brought in another three hundred and fifty local militia and our militia force of four hundred brought a total of nine hundred men. Most of them had rendezvoused at Sycamore Shoals up on the Watauga River and marched down together. Colonel Williams and Uncle Thomas conferred with the other colonels most of the evening.

The rest of us set up a rope line for our horses and picked out a place in the woods to sleep since we had no tents. Fortunately, we'd become experts at making good mattresses with pine needles. We then joined our new-found colleagues for supper. They were butchering and cooking some beeves. My, did that roasting beef smell good to us half-starved men.

After eating venison jerky and parched corn on the trail for three days, we were grateful to have roast beef even though we had no salt to go with it. But they also had tea and that was a luxury we seldom got when out in the field. With a good bed and a full belly, nothing much bothered me now but my hand-me-down shoes. They were so worn out, my toes on both feet showed through. Even my socks had worn off around the toes and I was forever stubbing and scratching them as I walked around.

The over-the-mountain men looked just like us in their hunting shirts and homespun trousers except many of them wore fur skin hats made from rabbits or raccoons. We mostly wore straw or felt hats, because of our warmer climate I reasoned. The mountain men were very amiable and just as eager to find and fight Major Ferguson's army as we were. Their units, like ours, consisted of boys and men of various ages. Uncle Thomas said it was good these over-the-mountain men mostly carried rifles like us.

"We can shoot straight for a fair piece," a big man in a coon skin said.

"What caliber are you shooting?" Uncle Thomas asked. "Fifty-four mostly."

"Same with us. Guess we can share ammunition if we need to," Uncle Thomas continued. "We surely appreciate you men for coming all this way to help out. I know what a hardship it is to be so far from home for so long."

"The fleas come with the dog, I reckon. We signed up to fight and we're mighty proud to do so, Colonel, no matter how far off the fight may be. When a British fancy pants threatens us and our womenfolk, we can't abide it."

"Ferguson's threats go against the grain, that's for sure," Uncle Thomas said. "Hopefully, we'll all get a chance to show him how we feel about him real soon."

"We aim to give him a whooping and git back home as fast as we can," the big mountain man said.

We spent the evening comparing battle stories, sharing news from our respective colonies and districts, and speculating how a battle with Ferguson might play out. We heard that General Cornwallis and more than two thousand British regulars battled their way into Charlotte and now occupied the Mecklenburg District. Later, after it turned dark, it turned cold.

"Looks like it's gonna be a two dog night, gentlemen," Collins said.

"For once I agree with you," Bobo winked at me. "You'd be right at home sleeping with dogs. Course, I'd rather have a pretty woman sleeping next to me."

"Bah," Collins said. "You're too young and dumb to have a woman. You haven't even found a sweetheart yet."

"No, but I expect to be working on it as soon as possible." I knew he'd already been working on getting a sweetheart and it was my sister. I admit she was a pretty one, but I doubt he knew what he was bargaining for … she could be mighty bossy when she took a mind to be.

We bedded down in our blankets with our clothes still on, including our hats.

The next morning, Joe Kerr brought intelligence that Major Ferguson was camped somewhere near the Cherokee Ford on the Broad River about thirty miles due east of the Cowpens. Once again, Joe was able to penetrate a Tory camp, curry favor, and gain valuable information about the enemy. I really admired Joe. He couldn't even talk and yet he provided more reconnaissance than any spy I ever heard of. He was everyone's hero. He'd wander into an enemy camp with a load of firewood and drop it by a campfire. Then he'd try to be helpful by currycombing horses or helping with some other chore. Inevitably, they'd offer him something to eat and once that happened, he had the run of the camp.

Our officers wasted no time in calling us to order. It rained steadily and we saddled our horses. Most of us wore heavy cloth coats with fringe on the sleeves and around the shoulders so the rain would drip off. Some of the men draped their blankets around their shoulders. We also wrapped cloths around our rifle locks to help keep them dry, but it didn't work very well. The cold water soaked my trousers and ran through my shoes like a sieve and the soles were falling off. We were a miserable lot. Even ole Dot seemed to be discouraged and walked with her head hung down like an old nag. Nevertheless, we rode steadily toward the enemy.

"This rain's getting to be a real toad strangler," Bobo said. "I'm wetter than a drowned rat," Collins said.

"That's a good thing for the rest of us," Bobo said. "You were beginning to smell to high heaven."

"If I had any soap, I'd just lather up." Quick as a wink, Christopher reached into his possibles bag and pitched Collins a small bar of soap. To our delight, he soaped his under arms on the outside of his jacket. Then he soaped his face and hands and let the rain rinse him off. He could be entertaining at times.

"I'm grateful to you, Collins," Bobo said. "I've been riding downwind of you and it was getting pretty dicey." None of us spent much time washing and such. We were more interested in staying alive and finding our next meal. Besides, it was common knowledge that too much washing led to all kinds of diseases.

We pushed east on the Green River Road toward the Broad River. I was excited about the prospect of engaging Ferguson again, but not at all excited about eating parched corn or nothing at all along the way. Once, both Colonel Williams and Uncle Thomas rode back along our regiment and talked to us as our horses walked along.

"We'll be making history today. Just do your job and we'll teach Ferguson to think twice before he threatens us again," Colonel Williams said. "Thomas, Christopher, and the rest of you, I know you'll make us proud." He tipped his hat.

Uncle Thomas said, "We won't have to worry about these Little River men, Colonel. They've been raised proper and they're Presbyterians!"

Our commanders chuckled as they rode on down the line. And we were proud to be Little River Presbyterians.

"Too bad Colonel Brandon didn't have some of Mary Dillard's cookies with him," Bobo said.

"Molasses. Those are my favorite," Christopher said.

"You don't know much about cookies," Collins said. "My Grandmother made the best gingersnap cookies this side of heaven. I can smell them coming out of that bee-hive oven now." He pretended to slurp with his tongue. "That's all I would need for breakfast, about a dozen of 'em."

For the next five minutes, we exchanged opinions about what made up the perfect breakfast since we had nothing to eat.

"It's not breakfast that worries me," Christopher said to me in private. "I just don't want to let my father down."

"Just because you're the colonel's son, doesn't mean you have to prove anything more than the rest of us," I told him. "He knows you're carrying your part of the load."

At noon, we crossed the Broad River at the Cherokee Ford and halted on the other side. We were exhausted, wet, and hungry. We needed the rest. A half hour later, word came down the line that a local Whig told our officers Ferguson was camped on top of Kings Mountain. It stood straight in front of us about ten miles away. The officers held a meeting and elected Colonel William Campbell, a tall red-headed Virginian, as the chief commander. Captain Jolly and Lieutenant Hollingsworth told us to travel in complete silence and that we were going to surround the small mountain. At the proper time, we'd all give a war whoop and start up the mountain.

"Now we're in for it," whispered Collins. "Those Tories will be shootin' down on us like we're fish in a barrel."

"No, they won't," I said. "We can surprise them if you can keep quiet. Besides, look at all those trees on the sides of these hills. We'll have plenty of cover."

"Tall people make the best targets, Collins, but don't worry," Bobo said. "Just stay close to us and we'll protect you."

"That'll be a fine thing to behold. I just hope you boys can keep up with me."

After several more miles of riding through the cold rain we halted at a plantation located on the banks of Buffalo Creek.

"I've got to leave you for a while," Sergeant Tate told us as he rode by. "This is my home and I'll be seeing my folks."

We knew he lived over in this direction, but had no idea this was his father's plantation. After a thirty-minute rest, another company of men from North Carolina joined us and Sergeant Tate rode back into our ranks.

"How was your visit?" inquired Lieutenant Hollingsworth.

"It was too short, but everyone's okay. Ferguson and his men camped at our plantation for two days and left yesterday. Those thieves stole my father's vegetables, chickens, and beeves. I've never seen him so perturbed. He'd be here with us if he weren't so old."

That's about all we could hear of their conversation before we mounted our horses and moved off toward Kings Mountain. We rode for another four miles or so and the officers halted the column. Somehow, a wet saddle makes you sorer than riding on a dry one. We all sighed with relief when we slipped off our mounts.

Lieutenant Hollingsworth and Sergeant Tate came over with final instructions. "Secure your horses here. Leave everything except your firearms. There won't be any need for swords in this fight. The brush is too thick. It's the rifles that'll do the work today, laddies," Hollingsworth said.

It was a good thing we didn't need swords because only officers carried swords to this fight.

"They've got British issue Brown Bess muskets which can't hit the broad side of a barn," Tate said. "Besides, they'll be aiming downward at a steep angle; they'll likely shoot their buck and balls over our heads."

"Yeah, but they can reload those muskets twice as fast as we can," Collins whispered.

I thought a lot about that large ball and three to six small balls that they would be shooting at us with each shot. Those muskets were more like shotguns than rifles. Their worst damage would be done at close range. Then I noticed my dilapidated shoes were flopping around so I removed them and pitched them into the brush. They wouldn't stay on my feet and would most likely trip me if I wasn't careful. My stockings were also torn to shreds, so I peeled them off and stood barefooted, ready for whatever came next.

"And consider putting a few balls in your mouths," suggested Sergeant Tate. They'll keep you from getting too thirsty and they'll be easier to get as you reload." We all knew about this trick already, but I suppose the Sergeant was getting a bit nervous and thought he should say something useful. I know I felt mighty anxious.

"Be quiet as you can and don't load your rifles until we get in position," Tate added. "We don't want any accidental shots to spoil the surprise."

"Just a couple more things," Hollingsworth began. "Remember to fire low and stay up with the line when we move up the mountain. If they charge us, don't panic. Just retreat and we'll start back up again as many times it takes to beat 'em. We'll not be shaming ourselves as them boys did down at Camden."

We tied our horses to a long rope attached to two trees so they could feed and move around some. Six or seven young boys, including Joseph Williams, stayed behind with them. I checked my shot bag and peaked in my powder horn to be sure it was still dry. The rainy sky spit big, cold raindrops, but it seemed to be slacking off some.

I slung my rifle over my shoulder, unsheathed my knife, felt its sharp edge, and replaced it in the sheath. Looking at it gave me some comfort when my nerves were on edge. It needed to be sharp to cut off the linen patches and you never knew when you might need it for self-defense.

Men do unexplained things just before a battle, and this fight would be the biggest one any of us had ever seen. Most of the men checked their weapons several times. I hung my powder horn around my neck, tied a strip of Lindsey cloth to my belt and waited for the order to move out.

Like Bobo, I wondered how many of us would be alive after this day. We stood huddled together there in the road.

"I don't know about anyone else, but I've never been so apprehensive as I am about this engagement," Collins said.

"I admire your honesty, Collins," I said. "I expect we're all feeling the same way, but are too embarrassed to admit it."

"I ain't scared a whit," Christopher said. "Like hell you ain't," Collins said.

"Would you like to fight about it, hook nose?" Christopher said.

"Ah, lay off, Christopher," Bobo said. "We're all on the same side here. I don't know if I'm bad scared, but I feel like throwing up."

"Don't worry about that, you haven't had enough to eat to throw anything up," Collins offered.

We stood there cold and dripping wet as we each thought about what we had to do. I mostly tried to think about Mother, the girls, and little Andrew. And I wondered if I had enough ammunition.

Collins broke the silence. "Where's your shoes, Thomas? You expecting a flood?"

"The darn things just fell apart. Figured I'd be better off without them. But I plan to get a British pair before the day's over."

"There you go, Thomas," Bobo said. Then he clinched his jaws in thought.

No one talked after that. We just adjusted our weapons and drained the water from our hats. Each person kept his own counsel. Sergeant Tate handed out small pieces of white paper for us to fold and tuck into our hat bands to distinguish us from the enemy. I tucked mine into two small slits in the front, since I no longer had a hatband. The provincials would be wearing red coats, but the Tories would look just like us so we needed a way to distinguish friend from foe.

"Move forward. Remember liberty and the women, liberty and the women," Captain Jolly said. We walked, four men abreast, up the road toward Kings Mountain. It looked more like a sizable hill to me, but I tried to put all thoughts out of my mind as we approached the enemy. As we got closer, I felt old man fear and his doubting ways enter into my thoughts. Here, I might get killed and I haven't even kissed a girl yet. As usual, I forced myself to think about John and what he would do. And I remembered my vow to avenge his untimely death. Whenever I thought of John's death, my fear turned into anger and anger is a much better emotion to feed when you're about to enter a fight.

It seemed like we arrived at the base of the mountain in just a few minutes although I knew it had to have been longer than that. We split into two large groups and surrounded the mountain which was about six hundred yards long and two hundred and fifty yards wide. The enemy camped in the meadow on top of the mountain. Before we got to our position, I saw two mountain men taking three enemy pickets back the way we'd just come. I assumed they had been taken by surprise since no shots had been fired.

"That's a real good sign," Bobo whispered. The soaked ground helped conceal our presence. And the fallen leaves made it easier for my bare feet.

At three o'clock the rain stopped. To my surprise I saw a woman in a long dress running down the hill toward us. Her long flowing brown hair was quite attractive, but she was wide-eyed and scared out of her wits. Uncle Thomas and Colonel Williams called her over and conferred with her.

"Thank God I reached you." She paused to catch her breath and kept looking over her shoulder up the mountain. "My name is Virginia Paul. I'm one of Major Ferguson's ladies. Two of us accompanied him here, but I want out so I've run to you."

"Woman, how do we know we can trust you?" said Colonel Williams.

"The major is wearing a bright red and white checkered shirt. And he'll be carrying his saber in his left hand. His right arm was wounded some time back and he can't use it much."

"That's good enough for me," said the colonel. "Pass on through our lines and thanks."

"And he'll be blowing a whistle to communicate his commands," she said as she walked on down the mountain toward the road.

I was loading my rifle when I heard our men open up with a loud, "Whoop, whoop, whoop," all down the line and we joined in. I quickly cut off a wadding patch from my linen strip and rammed it and the ball down the muzzle. In a few seconds we could hear our Patriots whooping all around the mountain. Almost immediately, we heard the Tory drums beating a call to action. Our line was two deep and each man poured dry powder in his pan ready to fire. Then up the mountain we went. The steep northern slope where I went up was rocky in some spots and full of brush in others. Numerous trees, mostly hardwoods, grew all the way to the top where the brush thinned out.

Lieutenant Hollingsworth stepped in line beside me. "I could use me a little dram of whiskey about now," he whispered to me. Then he straightened up his body to its full height and in a steady voice said, "Let's go get 'em, boys," he said. We began walking briskly up the hill and progressed about thirty yards before the enemy started shooting at us. Branches snapped and twigs dropped as their musket balls whistled overhead. At this distance, we heard the balls fly through the trees and brush before we heard the sound of their shots. We saw the smoke from their muskets and the report came a second later. It was a queer thing to observe, but I didn't have time to contemplate it. By instinct, I slipped behind a nearby tree and returned fire. When we heard a lull in their firing, Hollingsworth and I moved up to the next tree, reloaded, and continued to fire. Our officers fought right alongside us. Their presence provided us young privates some comfort, but we'd never admit to such a thing.

Colonel Williams rushed past me on his horse urging us to move forward. Just then, a Tory ball hit his horse in the jaw and that animal commenced stamping like he'd stepped into a nest of yellow jackets.

"Damnation, they've shot ol' Smoke," the colonel yelled.

Just before the horse slumped down, the colonel jumped off, stumbled a little and started up the mountain leading the rest of us.

"Forward, men. Let's take this hill!" he shouted and waved his sword.

My messmates fought alongside of me, but the smoke was so thick, I could only see a few people. We charged up the hill, but the enemy unleashed volley after volley of musket fire and we stalled. I stood behind one tree for a good long time and they fired at me until the bark was nearly all knocked off and my eyes got pretty well filled with it. As each shot exploded on the side of the tree, hundreds of tiny projectiles flew in every direction. These splinters felt like stinging nettles, but I kept loading and firing. One fellow shaved me pretty close when a bullet knocked a piece out of my gun stock.

My next shot wouldn't fire because the vent hole from the pan to the breach had clogged from so much firing. I quickly stuck the pick to it and fired away. Then I rushed up the hill to the next tree, loaded, and fired again. I forgot I was barefooted. I just thought about killing the enemy before they killed me.

I saw the summit and ran for it, but their bullets flew almost continuously and I ducked behind a boulder. As I caught my breath and looked around, I realized I stood between my own regiment and the enemy. I could see the paper in my colleague's hats below me and the green pine sprigs in the hats of the Tories above me. Then, to my surprise, the Tories fixed bayonets to their British-issued muskets and came charging down the hill. I bolted from my position and ran toward my company as they retreated swiftly down the slope.

Enemy soldiers yelled and came running at us fast. Thankfully, some of our men's rifles were loaded and they fired almost point blank on the enemy. This stopped their charge and they retreated to the top of the mountain.

"Re-form the line, men. Re-form the line," Sergeant Tate shouted. "Young, stay back here with the rest of us. You won't do any good by getting killed."

We started back up the slope, firing from tree to tree and boulder to boulder. I began to wonder if this battle would ever end.

Dead and dying Tories lay all over the hillside, but we paid them no attention. We were too busy trying to reach the summit and end the fight. Men on both sides fought for their lives. We fired indiscriminately now. We got to within forty yards of the top when they charged us again with those long bayonets. We couldn't fight against those knives with empty rifles so we quickly withdrew until we could stop and reload.

This is when Christopher got the scare of his life. As we retreated from this bayonet charge, he stumbled and fell and the Tories ran over him, but didn't stick him. One Tory actually stepped on his back as he lay prostrate on the ground. By the time he got to his knees, we fired and the Tories ran back up the mountain right past him. I guess they were too frightened to take the time to stab him. Christopher had escaped death twice in a matter of seconds.

"I believe I'll stick close to you today, Christopher Brandon," Collins said. "You've got the luck of the Irish with you for sure. Maybe some of it'll rub off on me."

"He's got a point there," Bobo said. "But don't let him have any of your luck, Christopher. In this fight you'll need all you can get."

We re-formed our line and started firing at the Tories who had regained the summit, about fifty yards away. All the shooting and shouting nearly deafened me. If there were any commands by our officers at this time, I couldn't hear them.

You'd think I would know what was going on with the battle, but

I only knew what I was doing and perhaps what the two people on either side of me were doing. That's the way it is when you're in a big fight. You don't have time to think about the whole battle. That's what the commanders do. I only had time to think about priming, ram-rodding the bullet down my barrel, and firing where I thought it would do the most good. Staying behind some cover was instinctive, I think. This went on for another twenty minutes.

In spite of the cool temperature, I sweated like I was putting up hay in August. Strangely enough, I wasn't tired. I was too excited, scared, and angry to think about being tired. One wouldn't think you could be experiencing three different emotions at the same time, but when you're in a battle, I swear it's true. The firing slowed down as the Tories moved back out of site. We were happy about this, since most of us ran low on powder and balls.

"Here they come again!" warned Captain Jolly. Although I couldn't see him, I knew the Captain's voice.

Once again, the enemy's charge stalled about halfway down the hill and they retreated back up to the summit as we shot at them. They fell all over the slope. Men fired their weapons and yelled and cursed. I stayed focused on the top of the hill, loading and firing at the enemy. I saw one British Provincial officer in a red coat and shot him through the breast. He slumped over and fell off his horse. "There's another one for you, John," I said aloud.

The enemy's ranks were thinning considerably. Up we went, this time we determined to take the mountain. I took a deep breath and rose up to begin a fifty-yard charge almost straight up and into their flaming muzzles of destruction. To my surprise, I saw Colonel Williams out front leading us to within twenty yards of the enemy. Then I saw him fall backward and slide down the slope a bit. I ran up to him and got there about the same time as his son Daniel. The Colonel was terribly wounded.

He rallied as Daniel lifted his head.

"For God's sake, men. Don't give up the hill."

I must have been crying because I remember wiping my eyes with my sleeve. He was our commander and he had always been our neighbor, a leader in our church, and he treated me like one of his sons. They took John from me, now Colonel Williams, I thought. I charged up the hill full of rage and left Daniel sitting there holding his father's head and stroking his hair.

This time we made it over the top and it was mass confusion. Everyone shouted, but I couldn't understand much of what they said. I heard about ten rifles fire in unison and turned in time to see Major Ferguson fall from his white horse and a cheer went up. His stallion bolted for a few yards and dragged him along the ground by his foot which had hung up in the stirrup. Several of his men threw down their weapons and stopped the horse. He looked smaller than I had imagined.

Out of the corner of my eye, I saw Jonathan Steen go down clutching his chest. I had no time to help him.

I was reloading my rifle when a Tory ran right toward me and threw his musket down yelling, "Thomas, Thomas, it's me, it's me!" After a moment I recognized the smoke-blackened face of my cousin, Matthew McCrary. "Mother made me side with the British because they've got my father in prison down at Edisto Island. She thought things would go better for us if I fought with them. But I'm on your side; I'm on your side."

"Get that sprig out of your hat, and pick up your gun and fight or get out of the way." I pushed past him. He just stood there in confusion.

A bullet whizzed past my head and I turned and shot the man who'd shot at me. His body twisted around and he fell flat on his face. I reloaded as fast as I could. My hands seemed to be detached from the rest of me, but I managed to reload anyway. As I looked for another target, a Tory officer fired his pistol at me. The bullet passed through my shirt, but didn't touch me. Then the Tory officer jumped from his wounded, staggering horse. "It's Cunningham," Bobo shouted. Sure enough, he came right toward me wielding his sword. I lifted my rifle and fired, but rushed the shot and only slightly wounded him in his left arm. He kept coming toward me with rage in his eyes. He closed within ten feet of me and raised his sword to strike.

"We surrender. We surrender," Ferguson's second in command yelled. "Drop your weapons, men. Drop your weapons."

Cunningham stopped, glared at me, and ran into a crowd of his men.

Partisans still flooded over the top of the mountain and didn't know the call for surrender had been made. As they saw the Tories and Provincials, they shot them. Others evidently knew about the surrender, but didn't care.

"Tarleton's quarter!" they shouted, referring to Tarleton's massacre of the surrendered Continentals led by Colonel Abraham Buford over at the Waxhaws last Spring. Watching those defenseless men die was an awful thing to see. The over-mountain men and some from our own regiment fired point blank at surrendered Tories. I still thought about Colonel Williams and how he must be dead by now, so I didn't really care what happened to those men, but I couldn't shoot them like that. I reloaded and looked for Cunningham, but couldn't find him. He seemed to have disappeared.

After a few minutes, the officers, including Uncle Thomas and Colonel Campbell, contained the men and the killing stopped. At the suggestion of an officer, we gave three rousing cheers. "Huzzah! Huzzah! Huzzah!" we shouted.

The dead and wounded lay everywhere. I couldn't believe my eyes and was elated we'd won the day for liberty. It was over. It took about an hour and a half for us to take that mountain, but we controlled it completely. Wounded men and horses moaned pitifully and the smell of death was everywhere. Once you smell the blood and gore of wounded men, you'll never forget it. Some of the blood was my own, I soon discovered. My left foot had a nasty gash on its side. No doubt I'd cut it on a rock coming up the mountain. I made a mental note to put some chewed tobacco on it as a poultice. "That's the best way to pull the evil out of a wound," my father always said.

Every minute or so I heard a rifle shot when someone put a wounded horse out of its misery; at least I presumed it was wounded horses they shot. I felt helpless in the midst of so much carnage and death, but I did manage to give a few wounded men drinks from my canteen until the water ran out.

I absently thought October 7, 1780, would indeed go down in history just like Colonel Williams had predicted. That's when I remembered his condition and hurried back to where I'd left him and Daniel.

Some troops had moved him to a wagon to transport him to a nearby farm home. I couldn't believe he still lived. He'd been shot at least twice, once through his body. I walked over to the wagon where he lay. He smiled up at me.

"Thomas, you and Daniel must look after Joseph now." "Yes, sir. You can depend on it, Colonel," I replied.

"Don't let any of the men worry about me. I am content that we've won this victory. It will signal the beginning of the end of our fight for liberty."

Colonel Williams then fainted. It was the last time I heard him speak. I left the wagon and went to take care of my foot which was beginning to throb something awful.

The next day, with Daniel and Joseph at his bedside, Colonel Williams died. This was the worst day of the war for us. We revered him as a fine person and the consummate commander. I cried over the Colonel and my heart ached for Daniel and Joseph

The rest of the regiment loaded up our dead and wounded into wagons. Jonathan Steen died and six or eight were wounded, including James Collins. A musket ball grazed his head, but he was expected to recover. Our officers then determined to leave the area since Cornwallis and two thousand men occupied Charlotte just thirty miles away. The officers told us to make haste in burying the dead and to meet back where we left our horses and be ready to leave at first light.

We left the Provincial and Tory dead where they lay, but some Tories buried Major Ferguson and his other lady, Virginia Sal, in a single grave just off the mountain top.

"The prisoners can bury their own," Colonel Campbell said. I watched them at this work and they didn't bury them decently at all. At most they just piled logs and brush over the bodies. I don't know what happened to poor cousin Matthew and never saw him again. He was one of them under that brush, I expect. Maybe Bloody Bill Cunningham was lying there somewhere, but no one found his body.

"The wolves, wild hogs, and cougars will make short work of those British lovers," remarked Sergeant Tate as he told us to prepare to move out. We picked up anything that might prove useful including balls and powder, clothes, and weapons. I grabbed a fine British-issued pistol and was quite proud of it. I then removed a good pair of boots from a dead provincial and they fit fairly well. My bare feet hurt and had scratches all over. I had a bandage over the deep cut on my left foot and it felt better. The dead man's socks felt good and helped stop what little bleeding that remained.

We took Jonathan Steen's body down the mountain and buried him in a small meadow beside the road. We dug a deep hole, wrapped him in his blanket and dropped him in. Two or three of us shoveled the dirt on him. I felt like vomiting. It could have been any one of us in that cold, dark hole. Captain Jolly read from his small Bible and Lieutenant Hollingsworth said a prayer of sorts.

"Death is so permanent," Bobo said as we walked over to find a suitable place to sleep. We'd be sleeping under the stars, but at least it wasn't raining.

"I can hardly believe Jonathan Steen is dead," I said. "I saw him take the shot that killed him. It was an awful thing, but I couldn't do anything about it. Everything happened so fast up there."

"I know what you mean. In my haste, I forgot to remove my ramrod and shot it right out of my rifle. It sailed up the mountain like a spear."

We talked long into the night about the battle, Colonel Williams, and Jonathan Steen. We pondered the meanings of life and death and we got very little sleep because the wounded men moaned all night.

At daylight, we picked up our accouterments, mounted our horses, and rode west toward the Little River District without any breakfast. We were concerned about our families and plantations since we'd left them vulnerable to Tory raids for over a week now. The over-the-mountain men were even more eager to get back to their homes since most of them had been gone for several weeks. Captain Jolly told us we'd captured around seven hundred prisoners, killed 157, and wounded another 163 men. Our losses amounted to twenty-eight killed and only sixty-four wounded.

We traveled back the way we'd come, to the Broad River at the Fondren Plantation just next to Sergeant Tate's home. We buried Colonel Williams there and all the men cried. Daniel and Joseph held up well. I invited them to join our company and mess, but they decided it would be best to stay with the company they'd been serving and Mary Dillard wanted them to camp with her, Captain Dillard, and Joe Kerr. I agreed that eating Mary Dillard's cooking was a wiser choice. Fortunately, the Fondren's gave us some provisions so we could have an evening meal. We cooked up some corn pone and bacon. I never smelled anything better in my life than that bacon.

A North Carolina regiment marched most of the prisoners to a Hillsborough prison camp. Those wounded too severely to walk or ride were carried to nearby homes to get well or die. We took about fifty of the most despicable and bloodthirsty Tories with us to be tried by military court in the field. Like everyone else, I believed in swift justice. At least we would give them a trial, which was more than they'd do for us if the situation were reversed. We all attended the court martial proceedings that afternoon. To my great delight, that vile pig Adam Steedham stood among the prisoners on trial.

After several hours of testimony and personal defense, the court ruled that ten men, including Steedham, be hanged. Uncle Thomas provided the convincing testimony that Steedham should die for his deadly deeds and he was the first to be put on a horse. With his hands tied behind his back, he darted his eyes this way and that, looking for someone to intercede.

"Thomas Young should have this honor," Uncle Thomas stated. "It was his brother, John, who was first to die in the raid this man perpetrated upon my troops."

No one argued with his proclamation. I climbed up on Dot and maneuvered her next to Steedham's horse. Someone handed me the noose end of a rope that was slung over a tree limb and tied to the trunk. I was never happier than when I placed the noose over Steedham's neck.

"Pull it real tight, Thomas," Bobo said.

"This is for my brother, John," I told him. He clenched his jaw and nodded curtly.

I pulled it tight as I could and backed away a few steps. His eyes bugged out in fright.

To his credit, he didn't say a word and looked straight ahead. But I could smell his sweat. Someone said a quick prayer for his soul and someone else swatted the horse. The startled horse jumped forward, the tree limb dipped, the rope stretched, and Steedham's body jerked in spasms for two minutes or so before he died.

"One down and one to go," I said aloud.

I felt like a long overdue score was settled and I wasn't ashamed at all. I was just disappointed that Bloody Bill wasn't stretching up there beside him. Strange as it sounds, it didn't help with my grief much.

We hanged eight other men that evening. One escaped and our guards escorted the other prisoners off to Hillsborough. I thought long and hard about death and dying that evening. In the end, I decided I'd much rather die on a battle field than be hanged. And war is pretty much a terrible thing, I was beginning to think.

At sunup, what was left of our army broke up and everyone went back to his respective State or district to protect his own folks. Again, we didn't eat any breakfast because we didn't have anything to eat. In fact, most of us hadn't eaten but one meal since the night before the battle over at the Cowpens and we were grumpy about it. Lieutenant Hollingsworth reminded us how much better off we were than the Continentals when they had to spend the whole winter up in Valley Forge with practically no food or blankets. We bid adieu to our new-found friends from over the mountains and started up the trail toward home.

"Sure wish I had somethin' good to eat," Collins commented as our mess rode along together.

"Just try sucking your thumb a little," Christopher suggested. "It might taste real good since you're so hungry."

"I might eat your fine leather belt, Brandon," responded Collins. "That's after I beat you with it."

"That'll be the day," Christopher said. "You're in no condition to fight just now and besides, you're twenty years old and getting slow."

"I doubt he's too old to whip you, Christopher," I offered, "but he probably has slowed down some. He didn't duck fast enough back there on Kings Mountain."

"I told him tall people make good targets, but he wouldn't listen," Bobo said.

About noon, Colonel Brandon led us up to a large pumpkin patch next to a pasture. "Here's dinner, gentlemen. I suggest you try roasting these pumpkins. We'll stop for thirty minutes."

To our delight, plenty of green pumpkins grew on the vine and we sliced and roasted a piece speared on a small stick right quick. "I never thought roasted green pumpkins could taste so sweet." I said.

"You must have a bad sense of taste, Young," Collins said while thumping one. "These things aren't even ripe."

"Just pretend it's good then, Collins," Bobo said. "And never thump a free pumpkin. It ain't polite."

As we sat around on the ground eating the pumpkins, Collins

pulled out a small bag of black tea he'd been hording without our knowledge. "I don't suppose you boys would turn down a cup of tea to go with your meal?" He smiled broadly with that crooked grin and big teeth flashing.

"I take back all the bad things I've said about you," Christopher said. "You are a prince and a friend indeed."

"It's nice to hear such kind words from you, Brandon. Now hurry and gather more firewood so we can boil some water before the colonel decides to move out. We scrambled off in all directions and built up the fire in less time than it takes to tell it. A cup of hot tea was heaven on earth to us in the backcountry. Lately, the only tea we could get came from sassafras roots. It was good, but a poor substitute to English black tea.

Bobo filled our small iron pot with water from a nearby rivulet. The water began to boil and Collins poured in a handful of ground black tea. I never smelled any tea as wonderful as that pot of tea. We all stood around the pot and soaked in the sight, sound, and odor as if it was our first time to experience such a thing. Just when the water turned dark brown, an old milk cow came ambling across the pasture toward the pumpkin patch.

"Look at that cow," Christopher said. "Hurry up and fill my cup," he said to Collins. "I'm going to have cream with my tea," he announced.

"Ha. This I'd like to see," Collins said as he poured the drink into Christopher's cup.

"Two shillings says you don't even get close enough to milk that cow," Bobo said.

"You're on," Christopher said as he walked off toward the cow. We could hear him talking softly to the animal as he approached her. She looked at him warily and stopped. He kept trying to sooth her so he could get a squirt of milk. He knew we'd never let him forget it if he was unsuccessful after making such a boastful claim.

Christopher walked around the cow slowly, talking all the time. The cow rolled her big eyes as she watched him. All of the men in our unit began to watch the event and voice encouragement. After a minute or two, Christopher closed in and placed his hand on her back. She flinched, signaling her skittish nature, but stood still. Then to our amazement, Christopher slipped his cup under her udder and reached under with his other hand to grab a teat.

"Mount up. Boots and saddles, boots and saddles," shouted Captain Jolly from the other side of the pumpkin patch.

In an instant, that cow jumped and kicked Christopher's cup of tea in a high arc through the air. She ran off across the pasture and into the woods like the devil had grabbed hold of her. We hollered at Christopher and everyone laughed unmercifully. We teased him for weeks about this delightful drama. After that, whenever there was any tea available, he always took it plain.

We reached our district the next day and dispersed to go to our homes for a few days. Everyone in the family was in good health except my father. His fighting days were over according to my mother, who knew more about doctoring than anyone else in our area. Father wasn't in any immediate harm, but could no longer sustain the physical demands of soldiering. Father explained that he would spend his time serving as a supply man, along with Absalom Bobo, for transporting food and provisions to our regiment. I enjoyed telling my family and Hank and them about the Battle of Kings Mountain. Father and Mother were especially pleased Adam Steedham had gone to his maker, but they were mighty sad that Colonel Williams was killed.

My time at home was brief as we were called back into camp, but I was there long enough for my mother to tend to my foot injury. She made me soak it in salted hot water three or four times a day and it healed nicely. At camp I heard that Major Joseph Hayes had been promoted by the South Carolina Provincial Congress to Colonel to replace Colonel Williams.

We also got word one thousand British and their Tories were marching toward our district. They resolved to kill us all for what we did to them at Kings Mountain. The over-the-mountain men and the North Carolina militia were all gone. There was no doubt our small militia wouldn't stand a chance against another large British force.

Kings Mountain by Dan Nance

BLOODY TARLETON

November 1780

It turned out that General Cornwallis ordered his troops to leave Charlotte and march south to Winnsboro after he heard about the defeat at Kings Mountain. He was afraid our over-the-mountain army might attack him at Charlotte where he'd had a devil of a time finding provisions and recruiting more Tories. That Mecklenburg area was filled with staunch Presbyterians and they didn't like being occupied by the British. Cornwallis reportedly wrote his superior and told him the place was nothing but a hornet's nest of rebellion. The Mecklenburgers were mighty proud of that distinction.

"Welcome back, men," Colonel Brandon addressed us as we re-assembled the Carlisle Company back at our main camp. "It appears Cornwallis wants revenge for our victory at King's Mountain and he's spitting mad that General Sumter whipped his Major Wemyss and his troops at a place called Fishdam Ford on the Broad River just thirty miles northwest of Winnsboro. Our spies tell us Cornwallis has pulled Colonel Banastre Tarleton back from chasing that old 'Swamp Fox' Marion and is sending him and his Dragoon Legion after us. It's our job to keep Tarleton from ravaging across the country. We'll join Sumter and attack Tarleton if we can fight from an advantage. Captain Jolly will send out some scouts and a squad or two to gather intelligence about Tarleton's movements."

Brandon paused, and then continued. "We must take this threat very seriously. Tarleton commands the best unit of the British army and his dragoons have never been defeated." Brandon paused again, then smiled, "Course, Tarleton hasn't met up with us upstate men either." Hats flew into the air. "Huzzah! Huzzah!" we shouted.

"Captain Jolly will be in command as usual and I'll be assisting Colonel Hayes with this operation. You all know Colonel Hayes and I expect you to afford him the same respect and allegiance you gave to Colonel Williams. That's it for now."

"Here we go again," Collins remarked as we walked over to our mess site.

"What's that supposed to mean?" asked Bobo.

"It means, I just about got my head healed and we'll be back fightin' before we know it," Collins replied.

"Don't that beat all," Bobo said. "Bloody Ban Tarleton is moving toward us and you aren't even excited?"

"He's not excited, he's scared," quipped Christopher. "He's concerned he might get another scratch on his hard head."

"I'm not afraid of fighting even though the odds are getting short on me," Collins said. "I just meant we should get ready for more starving and more saddle sores 'cause it looks like we'll be chasing around the country for a good while."

"Collins has a good point," I said. "This time I think I'll carry more food and especially some salt in case we find beeves like up there at the Cowpens. And I hope we do meet up with Tarleton and give him what he gave Colonel Buford over at the Waxhaws." I took off my hat and threw it on a folded blanket just inside my tent.

"Thomas, are you crazy?" asked Christopher. "You know it's bad luck to put your hat on a blanket." He leaned over and picked it up.

"Oh, I don't believe in that stuff," I said, "and give me my hat." "Have it your way, but I'm told Jonathan Steen did it just before we went up Kings Mountain. They buried him in that blanket you'll remember."

I snatched my hat from Christopher. "I'm not Jonathan Steen and I don't believe in superstitions. If it's your time to go, it won't matter whether you put your hat on a blanket or on a post. It'll simply be your time to go." I tried to sound confident, but in truth, Christopher's warning worried me some through the night and it prompted me to pray for protection. It is mighty tempting to get superstitious when you're fighting in a war.

We settled into our old camp comfortably and commenced to sharpen our knives, clean our rifles, and mend our shirts and socks. I checked all of our extra flints and used my little iron nap hammer to sharpen those that needed attention. Bobo and Christopher got busy melting lead into balls while Collins cooked some sow belly and corn pone for dinner. That bacon smelled good even though we ate it nearly once a day. It was good to have some time to prepare for whatever came next. Since we'd already had a frost or two, the ticks and chiggers were holed up and not bothering us. Those pesky lice were still a bother, but not as bad as they were in the summer.

I went with a few squads on patrol over the next three weeks, mostly to break up the boredom of camp life. My messmates and I did manage to make it over to Major Dillard's camp whenever we could. He'd gained a field commission. We told him we'd come hoping to get some of Mary Dillard's fine cooking, but it was really much more than that. We liked the company and enjoyed singing along with Daniel and Joseph Williams and anyone else who came around. We did our best to cheer up poor Daniel and Joseph. Joe Kerr couldn't sing of course, but he was fun to be with and to watch as he blew tones from the jug to keep time with the major's fiddle. Occasionally Uncle Thomas joined us and it was just like being at home on the front porch.

Somewhere around the middle of November, we noticed Joe Kerr had been gone for several days. This could only mean one thing; he was spying in an enemy camp somewhere. We speculated among ourselves, but never dreamed he would be at that moment amongst Banastre Tarleton and his famed dragoons and Tories. We shouldn't have been surprised. This handicapped, but courageous, partisan was a master spy.

Two or three days later the whole camp buzzed with activity just after sunup. Captain Jolly rode in from headquarters on the fly and dismounted. After conferring with Lieutenant Hollingsworth and Sergeant Tate, he stepped up on a stump and addressed the fifty or so men in our company.

"We just received word that Tarleton is headed up the Ninety-six Road toward us. He has close to one-thousand men consisting of his dragoons, elite infantry, and provincial infantry. He also has artillery." Jolly paused to let this information sink in. "But don't let this bother you. Colonel Brandon and Colonel Hayes are this moment conferring with couriers from General Sumter whom we will join to attack Tarleton at our first opportunity. We must be prepared to deploy at any moment. See to your provisions and weapons and be sure your horses are fed and ready to travel." With that, he remounted his horse and rode back toward headquarters.

"You heard him," Hollingsworth shouted. "Let's get prepared for a ride and a battle. Remember, we've whipped up on British regulars and dragoons afore, and I reckon we'll be doing it again soon."

Sergeant Tate quickly made the rounds and told all of us to pack up three days' worth of food and fill our powder horns and ball bags as much as we could. He didn't really need to tell us about the powder and balls. We always did this.

I was thrilled we'd get the opportunity to engage Banastre Tarleton, the most feared British officer in the whole Southern Campaign. He burned the plantations, schools, and even churches of Partisans and he gave no quarter to those who fought against him. I hoped Bloody Bill Cunningham would be with him and we could kill two nasty birds with one stone so to speak. It was appropriate that each of these foes were dubbed bloody as part of their name. In some ways Cunningham was even worse than Tarleton. At least Tarleton only killed soldiers. Cunningham murdered civilians if he thought they were Whigs. Even if they weren't, he killed people if he had a personal score to settle. We got word that he caught up with and killed the Continental officer, Captain Richie, who had beaten his brother to death. I had confused emotions over this news. I was glad to learn he hadn't died at King's Mountain. I would still have a chance to kill him myself. Also, I understood the justice in killing your brother's murderer, but my vengeance seemed more honorable than Bloody Bill's.

That afternoon, we joined Colonel Haye's regiment and rode out to rendezvous with General Sumter's men and some units from Georgia. We caught up with them at the Blackstock Plantation on the Tyger River in our Little River District.

Joe Kerr, with the interpretive help of Mary Dillard, told the commanders that Tarleton, in his eagerness to catch us napping, left his foot-bound infantry and most of his artillery behind. His dragoons and elite mounted infantry of regulars and provincials moved quickly up the Ninety Six Road directly toward us.

We stood by our horses all around Mr. Blackstock's outbuildings near the river ford waiting for orders. General Sumter and his officers rode past us in a trot. Sumter wasn't a big man, but he looked mighty tough, like an old hickory post. 'Gamecock,' they called him.

"Men, it's the twentieth of November 1780. I want you to remember this date as the day we handed Bloody Ban his first defeat," Captain Jolly said. "I expect to get orders any minute and this looks like as good a place for a fight as we'll find. Tarleton has out run most of his infantry and that'll give us a large advantage. If my thinking is right, we'll be positioned along this ridge and over on that hill by the tributary. Just hold tight here and I'll let you know what we're doing as soon as I learn it."

I liked Captain Jolly. He always framed things in a positive manner and he gave us confidence.

In less time than it takes to give your horse a good watering, Lieutenant Hollingsworth told us to secure our horses out of sight, position ourselves on the pine covered hill across the road, and hide in the underbrush. Tarleton and his men were only fifteen minutes away and coming fast. General Sumter decided to defend Tarleton's attack, taking advantage of the fact that Tarleton's force was divided.

We rode past the hill which overlooked the road from about sixty yards away and tied our horses in a wooded area near a small rivulet. Then we ran back up the hill as fast as possible. It was a small, but tall hill and it reminded me of an old Indian mound. Across a field and above the road which curved down to Blackstock's home and the river, I could see snipers positioning themselves in his cabins and out buildings. A Colonel Lacey positioned his mounted militia along the wooded ridge above the road and riflemen on foot stationed themselves up there too. There was a perfect open bowl formed by the ridge and the hill where we hid. I noticed Mary Dillard and Joe Kerr as they walked off the hill into thick woods which bordered a portion of the road and wondered what they were up to.

I didn't have long to ponder this riddle. A flagman signaled Tarleton was coming and everyone got prepared for the battle.

"Look there," Bobo said. "Here comes their famous colonel right at the head of his column." My heart raced from both fear and excitement.

"I hope we're not taking on something that's meaner than us." Collins said.

"Don't worry about it. Let's be ready to fight." I said. The famous Ban Tarleton looked like a leader indeed. He stood out from the rest of his men with his splendid green and beige uniform and the manner in which he held himself erect on his horse, confident and completely in control. He was tall, well built, and looked younger than I had imagined. His dragoons seemed to be without end as they came into view. These men also wore those imposing green uniforms with beige facings. The dragoons were followed by Tarleton's mounted infantry bedecked in bright red coats with blue accents and white waistcoats. They seemed to be numberless as they kept coming up the road rank by rank. My heart beat faster and faster.

As they approached Blackstock's outlying rail fence and came into the field, Sumter's militia opened fire from the ridge. At first there was mass confusion among the British Dragoons, but to their credit, they recovered quickly and formed a line of battle. Some of Tarleton's dragoons charged the line of men on the ridge above the road. We were too far away to engage, but we had a front row seat to the unfolding drama. Lacey's men joined the fray and the exchange of fire was unbelievably loud.

In the meantime, Tarleton's mounted infantry retreated back down the road into the trees, dismounted, and came running afoot to support the dragoons. Sumter's snipers then began firing from Blackstock's log buildings. Tarelton's Dragoons rushed down the road toward the buildings to hack at the men who just fired at them. Many of the snipers hadn't fired and waited until the dragoons where at almost point-blank range and opened up on them with a terrible volley. This staggered the dragoons and several fell to the ground. The rest retreated back up the road and some came across the field straight for the hill we occupied.

"Give 'em hell, boys," Hollingsworth commanded.

I balanced my rifle on a log and fired at the closest green coat I could see. The concussion and noise shook the earth since most of us fired at the same time. Green-coated men fell off their horses by the score. As I cut a new patch and spit out a new ball to reload, I saw the British infantry march from the woods into the field between the buildings and our hill. A general engagement commenced and we could no longer afford time for grand observation. We loaded, fired, and reloaded and fired as fast as we could. If the dragoons could reform a line and charge us with their swords when we were reloading, we'd be in bad trouble.

Fortunately, we outnumbered the British by three to one and we'd sort of trapped them in that bowl out in the open. Interestingly, ole man Blackstock's roosters crowed repeatedly even though it was long past daybreak. I suppose the gunfire riled them up. I imagined they were cheering for our side.

"A half turn to your left, men. Turn to your left and take their infantry," Captain Jolly shouted.

He didn't have to repeat the order. The infantry marched by two lines directly toward us. They were about thirty yards away when their first line kneeled and sent a volley at us. Instinctively, I pulled back behind the log and I could feel it shudder as their buck and ball loads smacked into it. I lifted up to fire back only to see their second line of men pointing their muskets at us. "Get down!" I shouted. Collins lay right beside me with his head down.

Bobo couldn't resist a comment. "It's better to eat a little dirt than get shaved again, huh, Collins?"

"You're darned right about that."

"Are you boys trying to talk 'em to death or shoot them?" I asked.

"On three," I said. "One, two, three." We all moved our upper bodies above the log and fired into their infantry. Men fell. Our militia along the ridge and those snipers in the barns and smoke houses also fired at these British troops.

The infantry broke under the enfilading fire and retreated toward the thick woods I'd seen Mary Dillard and Joe Kerr walk into before the fight began. The firing slacked off and I could hear shouts from our men. Tarleton and his dragoons rode off the field back down the road from whence they had come.

We watched General Sumter and his officer corps ride up past the Blackstock home presumably to watch Tarleton and his men retreat. Tarleton's rear guard stopped, turned, and fired muskets into the general and his men. Sumter slumped in his saddle and rode off with his officers' assistance. Tarleton's rear guard then turned about face and rode back after their retreating force.

A rousing cheer from the Partisans filled the air throughout the battle field. We jumped around and slapped each other on the back.

"We've won again!" shouted Bobo. "How about that."

"Better yet, we handed Bloody Ban Tarleton his first defeat." I said. "Collins, are you wounded anywhere this time?"

"He's not, but I burned my hand holding this danged barrel," Christopher intervened.

"I'm fit as a fiddle, boys. 'Cept for a little powder in my eyes, I never felt better in my life," Collins stated.

"Look at those wagons they left. Let's go see if they have anything worth eating in them," suggested Bobo.

Sure enough, Tarleton left two wagons full of provisions including hams, flour, beans, and tea. Better yet, he left both of the three-pound cannons he'd brought with him. These cannons were great prizes since no partisan militia units had cannons in the upstate backcountry. Colonel Brandon later named these cannons "Liberty" and "Independence."

Those roosters continued crowing as we walked over to look at the cannons. They shined in the sun and were beautiful to look at. Someone then shouted, "Would you look at that?"

"It's a woman leading a string of horses fifty or sixty yards long," another person exclaimed.

"That's no woman," Bobo said, "It is Mary Dillard. She's captured Tarleton's horses."

There she was, along with Joe Kerr, walking out of the woods by the creek. She led at least fifty saddled horses all tied to a single rope. She and Joe had gone into the woods hoping for such an opportunity. Tarleton's mounted infantry had tethered them to a long rope tied between two trees. During the height of the battle, she cut the rope at both ends and she and Joe led the horses across the creek in hiding until the battle was over. They exhibited great courage in this feat and we loved them for it.

I enjoyed thinking about Tarleton's horseless men walking all the way back to Winnsboro.

General Sumter had been shot with five or six musket balls and was in serious condition. The physicians attended to him. Colonel John Twiggs of the Georgia Patriot Militia replaced Sumter as commander.

Colonel Twiggs held a council with his officers after which Captain Jolly came over to our company. "We did very well today. We had only three men killed and five wounded. The enemy lost at least ninety men and seventy-five were wounded."

"Oh yez, oh yez," said several of our men.

"General Sumter is expected to recover, but has been removed from the field. Tend to your wounded and build fires at dusk. We want it to look like we're camped here for the night. But after dark we'll cross the Tyger River ford and disperse back to our own districts."

We made it back to our home camp without incident and a few days later I rode home. I couldn't wait to tell my folks about our great victory and the daring actions of Mary Dillard. Unfortunately, she stayed home after this engagement and we all missed her. Fortunately, Joe Kerr stayed with Major Dillard and kept up his spying activities as they were needed.

The closer I got to our place, the more I missed John and wondered if I'd ever get the chance to kill Cunningham. Little did I know that I'd be facing that cruel murderer sooner than I hoped.

A CAVALRY CHARGE

December 1780

Deep into December two things of note happened to me. Upon returning to camp, I was advanced in rank from private to cornet, just below the lieutenant's rank. This was a commissioned officer's position usually given to people who showed promise of handling greater responsibility. Sergeant Tate recommended the promotion before he went home on furlough to visit his gravely ill father. I was grateful to him and proud of the confidence he placed in me. I also was determined that my friendship with my messmates would remain strong even though I would outrank them.

The second thing of note occurred about the same time as my promotion. Thirty-nine-year old General Nathaniel Greene arrived in Charlotte bringing more Continentals into the south and took command from General Gates. General Washington highly favored General Greene who was known as a brilliant strategist. Greene immediately split his army. Virginia's famous General, Dan Morgan, who distinguished himself at the Battle of Saratoga and before that in the French and Indian War, took half of it to the upstate area. Greene ordered Morgan to, "Distress the enemy, afford protection to the partisans, and spirit up the people." General Cornwallis assumed Morgan and his brilliant cavalry leader, Lieutenant Colonel William Washington, would move to attack the British fort at Ninety Six. That's why he sent Colonel Tarleton to intercept General Morgan.

Morgan bivouacked at Grindal Shoals on the Pacolet River south of the Cowpens and we joined forces a few days before Christmas. I noticed right off the Continentals ate better food than we usually got. Of course, we militia ate the same fare as the Continentals at this camp and we liked it. We ate beef with spices and beans and potatoes. The Continentals seemed to be pretty good fellows, but we didn't mix much. They camped in one area near the river and our militia units camped in another, near some hardwoods. I admired them because they got very little pay for their efforts and their clothing looked as bad, if not worse, than ours. And they came from far off colonies like Maryland and Virginia. I was happy we stayed right here near home and were allowed to tend to our crops frequently.

The Continentals seemed to love General Morgan and most of them had fought with him at the Battle of Saratoga in upstate New York. They said the big, scar-faced general from Virginia was the real hero of that victory even though General Gates got the credit. They respected Colonel Washington too. Washington reminded me of Uncle Thomas in looks, although he was a little taller. He was light complexioned and sported red hair and a smile most times. Like Uncle Thomas, he was always eager for action.

We stayed camped there at Grindal Shoals through Christmas and none could go home since the enemy was rumored to be all about us. It was my first Christmas away from home. It would have been a very sad time except all of us were in the same boat so to speak. We sat around our fires, told family stories, and laughed together. And it helped to know our sacrifices were appreciated by our families.

Captain Jolly led the singing on Christmas Eve and each man was given a full tin of army issued grog. This was a welcomed surprise and it greatly lifted our spirits. Practically all the able-bodied men from our Presbyterian meeting house were there and we took comfort from one another. I vowed nothing short of war would ever keep me away from home for another Christmas time.

Colonel Washington learned that a party of about two hundred and fifty Georgian Tories recently plundered the countryside and wreaked havoc with the Whigs just north of their fort at Ninety Six. Colonel Brandon offered to reinforce Washington's dragoons with some of our best horsemen. He assured Washington that we would make good swordsmen and that our horses were strong in legs and long in stamina. We were issued swords and put into training immediately. I took to it like a duck to water.

In camp that evening my messmates and I jabbered about our day's training. Sergeant Tate, who had returned from furlough, joined us.

"Did you ever see anything as sharp as these swords?" Christopher asked.

"I'm surprised they let you children play with such sharp knives," Collins said.

"They knew we'd be fast and nimble," Bobo said. "Not slow and awkward like old lanky fellows."

I decided to change the subject, before Collins got perturbed.

"There you go trying to get our goats again, Collins," I said. "But that dog won't hunt tonight. We need to be reviewing what we learned today. We'll likely be fighting with these swords within the week."

"And we better be thinking about our horses," Bobo said. "We'll need to be picking out some young ones that have a lot of stamina."

"I'm sticking with ole Dot. She's strong, fast when she needs to be, and she is superb at cutting and turning."

"I'll be riding Crib," Christopher said. He's small, tough, and moves quick in close quarters.

"Just the kind of horse we'll all need," Sergeant Tate said.

We spent the rest of the evening discussing sword fighting maneuvers, horses, and who owned the fastest or the smartest ones. As I lay in my makeshift bed, I rehearsed in my mind how I would approach my foes with the sword. If I had time, I would make a false slashing move, then thrust for his mid-parts.

Two mornings later about two hundred of us mounted militia rode off toward the south in support of Colonel Washington's seventy light dragoons. The dragoons led the way and we hoped to catch the enemy by surprise. I rode at the front of our line, excited about the possibility of meeting up with Bloody Bill.

We caught up to a few of them about three miles from Hammond's store on Bush Creek north of the Ninety Six Fort and fairly close to my home place. Washington's dragoons captured two or three of them and learned their main body was camped near Hammond's store. We wasted no time in pursuing our objective. We stuck white paper into our hats and rode off at a fast pace. Anyone with a slow horse was left behind.

Colonels Hayes and Brandon led our regiment behind the Continental Dragoons. After a few minutes, the officers told us to stop and form a line just behind an open ridge, three ranks deep.

"The enemy is forming a line in the clearing on the next ridge," Colonel Hayes stated. "Form up the line and stay in position. Draw sabers!"

There wasn't time to think about any of those things you normally think about before a battle. I can only remember being excited about the chance to fight with a sword and pistol.

"Forward at a trot!" Colonel Washington yelled to his dragoons.

Off we went about twenty yards behind them. We saw the Tories hurriedly mounting their horses up on the next ridge about two hundred yards away. We trotted across a valley, splashed through Bush Creek, which wasn't very deep or wide, and started up the hill toward the enemy. I heard a loud shout from Washington's dragoons as they spurred their horses into a full gallop and raised their swords like mad men. We threw up a whoop ourselves and followed the Continentals as they dashed up the hill. Christopher's flaming red hair flew in the wind.

To my amazement the Tories, in their confusion, didn't fire a gun. We rode upon them lickety-split and engaged them in hand-to-hand sword fighting all across the open ridge. Some five hundred or more men slashed swords and fired pistols, all from horseback. I charged into the battle looking for an enemy. Swords clanged, pistols fired, and men grunted.

I heeled Dot and rode in fast, unseating a man in short order. He was an older heavy-set brute who seemed surprised that someone my age could best him in a sword fight. It wasn't all that difficult. My foe was slow and defended against my first slashing feint which came from the left. My quick thrust to the right impaled him and he fell backward, wide eyed, sliding off my sword.

"Watch out, Young," I heard someone shout. I looked behind me just in time to see Sergeant Tate slice through a Tory's wrist as he slashed down toward my head. The Tory's hand and sword bounced off the back of my horse and fell to the ground. The man screamed and grabbed his handless arm, but it did him no good. Sergeant Tate thrust his sword clean through the man and he fell to the ground.

"You saved me, Sergeant. Thanks," I said.

"Let's get another one," Tate said as he rushed off toward an enemy.

I turned Dot to find another opponent and saw a Tory slash Lieutenant Hollingsworth across his chest. He was too far away to take with the sword, so I shot him with my pistol. The man flew off his horse as if he'd been hit with a pole ax. He tried to raise himself upright, but couldn't do it. Blood stained his shirt on both sides.

Some movement on my left caught my attention. It was a fresh group of about ten Tories rushing into the fight from our rear. "About face," I yelled. "Rally to the rear. Rally to the rear." Fortunately, several of our militia, including Bobo and Christopher, turned with me to face this assault. When the charging Tories saw their surprise attack had been discovered, they peeled off in two directions. One of the men was clearly Bloody Bill Cunningham. By instinct, I pointed my pistol at him and pulled the trigger, but it wasn't loaded. Two or three of our men shot pistols at them to no avail, but Bobo shot a man who fell to the ground like a bag of potatoes and he bounced causing a cloud of dust. Bobo fought better with a pistol than with a sword. I started after Cunningham, but Bobo shouted at me to stop.

"You can't take on five men by yourself, Thomas."

He was right and they were too far ahead for me to catch them anyway. All I could do was watch Cunningham ride out of sight and curse my luck.

Then it was all over. The enemy around us, what was left of them, threw down their weapons and surrendered. The rest of the Tories rode off the field. I grabbed Lieutenant Hollingsworth's reins and led his horse over to a tree so he could dismount. He had a deep cut across his lower chest and stomach, but his intestines weren't sticking out and he didn't seem to be dying. His red gash opened a little every time he breathed and it was a ghastly sight.

"Looks like he got you pretty good, Lieutenant," I said.

"Ey, you're right about that, Young. I just hope my innards stay put 'till someone can sew me up." He sat there on his horse in confusion, as if he didn't know what to do. "I could use a good stiff drink about now."

"I'll bet the surgeon will take care of both requests when we get you back to camp," I told him. "Give me your reigns and I'll get you over where you can be tended to."

Bobo rode over and helped me get him off his horse. We sat him up against an oak tree and gave him his canteen. "Bobo will stay with you until I can get someone back up here with a wagon," I said.

"Many thanks, boys. God bless ye."

Our first cavalry charge was exhilarating to say the least. Captain Jolly wrapped up Lieutenant Hollingsworth's wound, but said the regimental surgeon at Morgan's camp would have to sew him up. We all knew his fighting days were over for several weeks, if not permanently.

Captain Jolly told us that several of the Tories escaped, but the majority were killed, wounded, or captured. The Captain said he'd heard we killed or wounded one hundred and fifty of the enemy. Luckily only a few of our men were wounded and none were killed. No one saw hide nor hair of Bloody Bill after he fled from the field. He was good at escaping trouble.

We transported Hollingsworth to our camp with a wagon brought over by a local partisan. We laid him on a pallet and the surgeon told him to drink a full cup of whiskey before sewing him up. After the procedure was over, Hollingsworth said he enjoyed the surgeon's whiskey more than the surgeon's needle. They transported the lieutenant home the next day. At the same time, Sergeant Tate was called home. His father had died.

A few days later, when we were back at Grindal Shoals, a courier arrived and told Colonel Washington that a Loyalist group under South Carolina Brigadier General Robert Cunningham, Uncle of Bloody Bill, had seized the late General James Williams' house, chased off his widow and three young children, and fortified the place as a Tory garrison. This news incensed those of us who fought for Colonel Williams.

"Haven't the Tories done enough to the Williams family?" asked Major Dillard.

"I know this much," Colonel Brandon added, "It's past time for it to stop. Joe, we need to be at the front of this engagement."

"Agreed. Let's talk to Colonel Washington," replied Colonel Hayes. He turned to Major Dillard, "Prepare the men to move out."

I fumed over this circumstance. The Cunningham's lived practically next door to the Williams and old man Cunningham could have used his own place as a headquarters.

Captain Jolly came over to me. "Young, we need to replace Lieutenant Hollingsworth. You made yourself proud today and we think you're the man for the job. Colonels Brandon and Hayes have commissioned you as lieutenant."

I was very much surprised, but pleased at this commission. "Thank you, sir. I'll do my very best."

"I know that. Now tell the men with the best horses to get prepared for a fast ride to liberate Mrs. Williams and her children."

Evidently, Colonel Washington agreed with our interest in rescuing the Williams family and their plantation, locally known as Mount Pleasant. About forty of us who owned fast horses, along with ten dragoons, peeled off and rode across country toward the Williams place. We rode hard for about three miles and came up through the woods west of the home along Mud Lick Creek. We sent scouts to determine if the Williams's Mill was occupied by Provincials or Tories. They returned to tell us only Mrs. Williams and her children occupied the place. They'd fled there for protection when General Cunningham and his British lovers arrived.

Mrs. Williams cried when Daniel and little Joseph Williams rode up to her. The large rock grist mill offered plenty of room for storage and people. It would have made a better fort than their house, I thought. They milled very little grain there these days. Most of the grain was stolen by the Tories or requisitioned by the Partisans before it could ever be ground since they needed it for their horses. I recalled going to the mill several times with my father. Colonel Williams always had a keg or two of peach brandy to share with his customers.

"That's how he got so many customers," my mother would always say. I was allowed a small amount on each visit, but never enough to be "in the cups" as we said about drunkards. Seeing Mrs. Williams and her sons reunite made me a bit homesick.

After a five-minute consultation there by the rock mill, our officers decided to ride by columns straight to the Williams house. I hoped Bloody Bill would be there. There were only about ten horses in the corral. We caught the Tories completely by surprise and Colonel Hayes told them to surrender their makeshift garrison within five minutes or we would attack. We had them seriously outnumbered and were confident we could wipe them out.

"Give us ten minutes and we'll surrender," Cunningham requested.

Colonel Hayes complied and we dismounted. In the meantime, Cunningham and his troops managed to slip out the back of the house through the root cellar and escape on foot. I was sorely disappointed if Bloody Bill had been there or not. That evening we left the Williams family with ten militia guards to protect them and rode off to the Grindal Shoals camp to rejoin General Morgan. Daniel and Joseph stayed behind with their family.

Unknown to us at the time, our next engagement would be more terrifying than any we'd seen before.

MY SEVENTEENTH BIRTHDAY

January 1781

We returned to Morgan's encampment at Grindal Shoals and remained there for a little over two weeks. The wind blew steadily from the north and frost covered the ground nearly every morning. Fortunately, we were well provisioned with beef and we slept with double wool blankets. A post rider came by one Friday and I received a letter from my father. All was well at home, but everyone stayed on the alert for Tories, including us. I went on several neighborhood scouting trips, but Tories were becoming scarce since we'd won the past several battles in the upstate backcountry.

I did run into two Tories of note while out fishing on the river on an unusually warm afternoon. I planned to catch a smallmouth or two for supper, but I caught trouble instead. Two Tories from my community walked up behind me and caught me by surprise. They were Captain George Littlefield and Sergeant James Kelly. Littlefield leveled a pistol at me, but Kelly carried only a large hunting knife. I always liked James and I was surprised he became a Tory. George Littlefield was some kind of kin to him so I guess that's why he turned into a loyalist. Almost no one liked George Littlefield, even before he became a Tory. We all knew him as a bully and a boastful man.

"Would you lookie here what we've found," Littlefield said. "Colonel Cunningham will be happy as a toad about this. Hand over the pistol, Young."

"Not on your life, Mr. Littlefield."

"Better do what he says, Thomas. You all whipped us there at Hammond's store and the captain ain't in no mood to be patient with you," advised Kelly.

"That's for damned shore." Littlefield said as he thrust his hand for the pistol in my belt. Instinctively, I stepped back, grabbed his wrist and pulled him forward and to the side of me. His momentum threw him off balance and he sprawled into the river firing his pistol in the air and dropping it as he struggled to regain his balance. Kelly couldn't hold his laughter. I pulled my pistol, cocked it and pointed it right at Littlefield's face.

"If you don't run out of here, I'll blow your head off," I told him. "And James, throw that pig sticker into the river." He threw the knife into the river. Littlefield crawled out of the water, scowled at Kelly, and the two of them stomped off through the woods. "Just you wait, you peckerwood. I'll even the score. Your day's coming!" Littlefield shouted. "We fixed your brother for good and you'll be joining him soon."

His sneering face and scraggly beard reminded me of a rat. "That may be so, but it won't be today," I said. I had a strong inclination to shoot Littlefield, but he was disarmed.

After that, I decided to pick a fishing spot closer to camp.

At the Shoals camp we spent time practicing our marksmanship and learning new saber fighting techniques. We sometimes practiced on straw men which looked like poorly made scare crows tied to poles so they would be at the height of a man on horseback. I enjoyed this training and we had plenty of laughs at each other as we sometimes missed the target. Bobo even fell off his horse once. It embarrassed him, but he took our ribbing in good sport.

Rumors flew everywhere concerning Tarleton's whereabouts. We hoped he would show up soon since we itched for a chance to get rid of him and his dragoons for good. We knew if we could get the British out of the backcountry, the Tories would have to behave themselves or we would run them out too.

On the fifteenth of January, Colonel Brandon told us in an officer's briefing they had reliable intelligence that Tarleton was approaching our position. Major Dillard had assigned Joe Kerr to reconnaissance duty and once again, Joe came through.

"Finally," I said to my old messmates, "we'll be able to finish Bloody Tarleton for good."

To my disappointment, our commanding officers told us to strike the camp early the next morning. Tarleton was marching to cross the Pacolet River above us and General Morgan decided to retreat up the mountain road before that could happen.

"Lieutenant Young," asked one of my soldiers, "why are we retreating? Don't we have enough men to smash Tarleton?"

I ran my fingers through my hair thinking about my response. "General Morgan knows what he's doing. Just hold on; I'm sure you'll soon get enough fighting to suit you." In secret, I had the same question in my mind, but as an officer, it wasn't proper to ask it.

We traveled hard all day, not stopping for a mid-day meal. We ate parched corn and pemmican from horse back or during one of the infrequent breaks when we let the horses blow. We were all thin from scarce rations and hard living. But we'd been toughened up from living out in the elements and riding horses till the seats of our breeches wore out. I patched mine with a double fold of what was left of my last shirttail. Most of the men did the same. We used what we called a "house wife" which was just a bag of thread and a needle for mending clothes. The good ladies from the Duncan Creek meeting house sent each of us this little necessity. They'd put them together for us one Sunday afternoon, my mother wrote.

I quickly learned the ropes for being a lieutenant and I rather liked it. I especially liked knowing something about what was going on and I enjoyed being treated more or less as an equal with the officers. The officer's mess, where I now ate my meals, presented the same food as before, but it tasted better because we usually had spices with our food. I missed my old messmates though and still stayed in close touch with them.

At sundown, we arrived at the same place we first reconnoitered with the over-the-mountain men back in October. We were back at the Cowpens. Several North Carolina and mountain-based militia regiments were already camped there waiting for us. I realized I shouldn't have doubted our wise old general. It appeared he'd had a plan for taking on Ban Tarleton all along. This circumstance and the thought of having roast beef again pleased me greatly. Captain Jolly told me to unsaddle my horse and come over to Morgan's headquarters for a briefing.

At the briefing, General Morgan explained he'd chosen this place because it gave our army an advantage. The open area sloped gently toward the east and was surrounded by intermittent trees thick enough to provide some protective cover, but not too thick for maneuvering troops.

"We'll make our stand here," the General continued. "The terrain is in our favor, we have ample provisions, and I expect more militia reinforcements throughout the night. Our scouts tell me Tarleton is pursuing us about six hours back. We'll have plenty of time to prepare a proper reception for him and his legion of bloody-backs."

The general's words and confidence inspired me and all who heard him. We were more than ready to do our part, especially my company. Captain Jolly and I left the hour-long meeting full of excitement and began walking back to our camp when Colonel Brandon called to us.

"Benjamin. Thomas. Hold up a moment." We stopped and he caught up. "We need the two of you to step up a notch. Colonel Hayes and I are promoting both of you again. As you know, we're thin on officers and we'll need all we can muster tomorrow. Colonel Andrew Pickens requested Major Dillard be reassigned to command his reconnaissance unit for the entire upstate area. Joe Kerr will go with him, of course. Benjamin, you're assigned the field commission of major to replace Dillard. Thomas, you'll replace Benjamin as captain of your company."

I don't know how Captain Jolly felt, but my head swirled. I'd only been a lieutenant a short time and here I was expected to assume the role of captain. It was a wonderful honor, but quite intimidating to a sixteen-year-old. Then I remembered that tomorrow was my seventeenth birthday. I'd grown up a lot in the past eight months.

I would assume command of the company and Jolly would assume command of three captains with companies including mine. Colonel Brandon explained that Sergeant Tate, who had returned from burying his father, would become captain of the Duncan Company and Bobo would assume my lieutenancy. Changes came quickly. Just like that, Jolly was a major, I was a captain, and Major Dillard and Joe were whisked away from us.

Thankfully, they also promoted Christopher as Sergeant or he would have been very disappointed. We thanked the colonel and walked briskly back to the tent we shared to discuss our new roles and, hopefully, find some beef steaks. We held heavy thoughts on our minds that night. Tomorrow we'd face the most powerful army in the world. We knew Tarleton and his dreaded dragoons would be demons on the field after their stinging defeat at the Blackstock Plantation.

When Colonel Brandon left, I confided in Jolly.

"I've only been a lieutenant for a few weeks. How am I supposed to be a captain all of a sudden?"

"Don't worry about it. You've got good instincts. Just remind the men they're fighting for liberty, their mothers, and sweethearts … they'll fight for you. They have confidence in you already and they know you'll be looking out for their best interests. And don't forget, our commanders also have confidence in you or they wouldn't have selected you."

"Thanks."

"You're welcome. Now let's get back to the men and get organized for tomorrow. I've got about the same time to learn to become a major as you do to become a captain."

Later that evening, Colonel Brandon asked Major Jolly and me to select about twenty of the best riders and saber fighters from my company to act as a support unit for Colonel Washington's Light Dragoons. The men were happy about this because we'd fought with Washington at Hammond's Store and admired his common sense and his courage. And it was an honor to fight under a Continental officer who was a cousin to General George Washington, commander of the entire Continental Army.

We were told to select any horse not belonging to a dragoon or person of higher rank since we would need to employ the best horses during the fighting tomorrow. I stuck with Dot since she was as good as any and better than most other horses and I trusted her completely. We issued new swords to men who needed them. It was a cold night, but our militia sat around their fires talking for most of it. Some wrote letters, but most melted lead for ammunition or prepared their guns, knives, and swords for battle.

General Morgan was about fifty years old, but tough as a boot. I don't think he got any sleep that evening because he moved from unit to unit talking with the men, especially the militia. He knew the militia would be a primary key to victory and he wanted to boost their confidence and courage. He really had no authority over us since we were basically back-up volunteers to his Continentals, but we were all ready to follow him as he commanded.

Morgan was the first Continental general I ever knew and he was much more personable than anyone expected. Colonel Brandon told us Morgan's nickname was "Old Waggoner," and that he fought with the British in the French and Indian War and received four-hundred lashes for accosting a British officer. He had ample reason to hate the British ever since. Few men could survive that many lashes. He called the British "Bloodybacks" because they lashed their soldiers to discipline them.

Morgan moved among the volunteers, sharing in their meals or tea around their camp fires. He joked with them about their sweethearts and told them to be in good spirits. He told the militia infantry he would lay the whip to Ban Tarleton tomorrow and if they would fire just three times, that would be all he'd ask of them. "We'll take that stiff-rumped Brit down a notch or two if we all do our jobs," General Morgan said. "He thinks you militia will all run off and that will be his undoing. When we're victorious tomorrow, you can return to your homes and the old folks will bless you and the girls will kiss you for your gallant conduct." He took a drink of water from his canteen and everyone remained still until he finished. "I'm an old dog at this game gentlemen and I can smell victory a day off. Just remember, we're all fighting for liberty, boys. We're fighting for the cause of our time."

I decided that if the commanding general could do all this, I could do my part as well. I also walked around and talked to the men of my company who would be on horseback with Major Jolly and me tomorrow. Colonels Brandon and Hayes would take command of the rest of our men to fight as infantry.

"All we have to do is support Washington's dragoons," I said. "Where they go, we go. You're good swordsmen and the best horsemen in the company. And we'll be moving most of the time, not standing there in the open making easy targets." They seemed pleased with this and other assurances I offered them during that dark cold night. I knew I was younger than most of them, but out here just before a battle, age makes little difference. Their confidence in you is all that matters.

It was late, but practically no one slept because of the impending battle and the cold air. I strolled over to my old messmates to chat.

"Getting any sleep, fellas?"

"Golly no, Thomas. How do you expect us to sleep on a night as cold as this?" asked Bobo. "But it's sure good to see you. Congratulations on another promotion."

"Yeah, at this rate, you'll be colonel by summer," Christopher said.

"Ha! That's not likely, but I'm proud you and Bobo have moved up the ranks."

"Look who's talking, Sergeant Brandon," Collins said. "Christopher would probably be a major by now, but he has to learn to quit trying to fight the British Army all by himself," Bobo said.

"There's truth in that," Collins said. "I'd be captain by now if I'd wanted to." He pitched a stick on the fire. "Except I don't want to ruin my reputation by becoming an officer." He flashed that toothy, crooked grin at us.

"That's as good an excuse as any," Bobo said. "Truth is you don't want the extra work it takes to be an officer." Collins smiled and nodded.

I sat down by their small fire. "Do you know where your assignments are in the morning?"

"Yeah, we know all right," Bobo stated. "Collins and Christopher and I'll be standing with the rest of the company with Colonel Brandon on the second line. I sure wish you'd let me come with you and the dragoons."

"It's not up to me. I suppose the commanders needed at least one courageous man to set the example for the rest of the company," I told Bobo.

"Why would they say that?" Collins said, feigning surprise. "I'm going to be there, aren't I?"

"That you are, Mr. Collins. Please forgive the oversight. And I'm sure you'll do your best to protect your messmates."

"Now that Bobo's the Lieutenant and Christopher is the Sarge, they'll have to protect me."

"You've got a point there," I said.

I wanted Bobo to be with me, but his saber skills were not particularly good and it left him too vulnerable as a cavalryman. He sensed it, I think. Christopher was more than capable as a cavalryman, but Uncle Thomas requested that he fight alongside him.

"I'll be fine with this bunch, Thomas," Bobo stated. "Just take care of yourself. We don't want anything to happen to our new captain."

"Ah, nobody's worried about that. Young's too tough to kill," Collins said. "But don't do anything stupid. And that goes for the rest of you."

"Are you going soft on us, Collins?" Christopher asked. "Or have you had a premonition?"

"No to both questions. I've just kinda gotten accustomed to having you boys around and I'd like it to stay that way."

"We'll all be just fine if you keep your head down and if Christopher don't try to be a hero," Bobo said as he winked at me.

"I won't do anything heroic unless I get the chance," Christopher said. "I really wish I could be up on that front line with the sharpshooters so I could get me some officers … I guess you heard old Squire Kennedy volunteered to be one of the sharpshooters tomorrow?"

"They couldn't have picked a better shot," I said. "Too bad William's not here. They'd make a great father–son team."

Bobo pointed through the trees. "Speaking of father–son teams, here comes Colonel Brandon."

We all stood at attention.

"Sit down, please. I wish you the best tomorrow and I want you to know how much I've come to depend on you. And," he looked straight at Christopher, "how proud I am of you." He slapped Christopher on the back. "See you in the morning." After a few more encouraging words, he turned and walked toward the next camp fire.

The boys and I talked on for over an hour. I felt most at home being with these friends and we gained confidence from each other. I stood up to leave. "Don't forget to put new paper in your hat bands," I said as I bid them goodbye.

"Keep your powder dry," Bobo said.

I walked back to where Major Jolly and his three captains, including me, were camped.

"I see you've been making the rounds with your troops, Thomas. That's a good thing," Jolly said.

"They're itching to whip Tarleton and their only complaint is the cold weather," I said. "I'm grateful it's not raining like when we camped here before riding to King's Mountain."

"Ha. If we had any precipitation tonight, it would be sleet or snow," Captain Tate chimed in as he pulled a blanket closer around him and threw a big log on the fire.

"You're right about that," Jolly said. "Let's hope it warms up quick in the morning so the men can keep their thoughts on the battle rather than the temperature." I grabbed my blanket and sat on a log beside the fire. The darned pine wood smoke blew my way and I had to keep moving up and down the log to keep it from pestering my eyes and nose.

"Smoke always follows beauty," Tate said. "I hope that's true," I said.

Major Jolly told us that General Morgan was laying a trap for Tarleton and his army and he had the utmost confidence in his plan. Except for a few trees, there was no underbrush in the battlefield because it was burned off each spring to encourage new grass to grow for the cattle brought there. The field had an almost imperceptible rise toward our position on the west. Just over the rise a swale dipped deep enough for cavalry to wait without being seen by the enemy. This is where my cavalry would be with Colonel Washington until deployed into action against the British and their Tory cavalry.

Morgan planned to place three lines of men across the field about one hundred and fifty yards behind each other. His forward line would contain about one hundred and fifty sharpshooters who were instructed to shoot the British officers and then retreat behind the second line of militia volunteers. Five hundred militiamen were instructed to fire three shots and retreat, along with the sharpshooters, behind the third line consisting of about three hundred hardened Continental regulars. About two hundred of us cavalry troops stood ready behind the Continentals. We carried only swords, knives, and a few pistols because we'd be fighting mostly hand to hand.

"British officers hold little respect for volunteer militia because they ran like cowards at Camden," Jolly said. "General Morgan is counting on the British to hold this contempt for them here at the Cowpens. Hopefully, as each of the two volunteer lines retreat, the British will think we've been overthrown and will be surprised as they run directly into our Continentals. Washington's Light Dragoons and our mounted militia will strike the enemy wherever needed and eventually surround them as they're fighting off our Continentals."

Our pickets were placed out as far as three miles, east along the Green River Road. And we had scouts out in every direction to avoid a surprise attack. An hour before sunup we woke up the camp and moved men to their designated places. Tarleton and his legion marched straight for us and the apprehension was strong among all of us.

We ate no breakfast this morning. The cold penetrated our clothing and we slapped our hands together to keep warm. I kept reminding myself that we had a good battle plan and a little more than one thousand men, just about as many as marched with Tarleton. We also had the two three-pound cannons we'd captured from Tarleton at the Blackstock Plantation. My men and I stood beside our horses in the swale alongside Colonel Washington's Light Dragoons. General Morgan sat on his horse just above the swale along with Colonel Pickens and Colonel Washington. Colonel Washington's African orderly sat on a little brown horse beside his master. They were about ten yards in front of me. The rest of us stood by our horses to preserve their strength until the battle began.

Predictably, the British drove in our pickets just before sunup. We heard a few shots off in the direction of Tarleton's army. A short time later, one of Washington's lieutenants rode up to brief General Morgan. Great clouds of steam lifted from his black horse.

The man saluted the general. "Nicholas Coble, sir. They're not but a fourth of a mile from us and coming fast." Vapor shot from his mouth in the crisp morning air.

"That means they've been marching most of the night," Morgan glanced at Colonels Pickens and Washington.

"That's a good thing for us. At least our men are rested," Pickens replied.

"Who was in the lead, Lieutenant, his cavalry or his infantry?" Morgan asked.

"His cavalry, sir."

"That's what I expected. They'll not attack yet." The general wiped his nose with a kerchief. "They'll have to wait for their infantry to catch up. Did you lose any men?"

"They captured one of our scouts, sir."

"Sorry about that, Lieutenant, but I'm happy they only got one of your men. How far back were the infantry?"

"About a mile I'd say, sir."

"Colonel Pickens, Colonel Washington, it's time to pull on boots and jump in saddles. Boots and saddles, men," he ordered. "The enemy will be here within ten minutes. Have the drummers play the long roll." Upon receiving the order, drummers played continuous rolls to alert everyone to the impending conflict. We mounted our horses and saddles and stirrups creaked loudly, but it was a comfortable, reassuring sound.

General Morgan continued his conversation with the officer of the scouts and pickets.

"Lieutenant, ride forward and remind the sharpshooters to shoot only the officers, any man on horseback, or anyone with epaulets on his shoulders." Coble rode off with the message.

After hearing this exchange, a shiver went up my spine and my mouth got dry. I forced myself to remember my brother and my family and that I was now an officer. I took a good long drink of water from my canteen and double checked my pistol to be sure it was still primed and ready for action. Then I lifted my knife a little, felt the sharpened edge, and replaced it. "Brace up, men. We've got a chance to be heroes today." I heard myself say this, but it didn't seem like my voice. I was grateful it didn't crack into a squeaking sound as it was prone to do when I was anxious. We could hear their drums now and my heart beat rapidly.

The sun peeked above the rise and a little wind blew up when we saw the first line of British Regulars come into sight. They walked briskly to the beat of their drums coming toward us in their bright red uniforms. I stood up in my stirrups to see well. It was the most beautiful line I'd ever seen. A misty fog dissipated and their red and white uniforms, straight lines, and colorful flags flapping in the breeze presented an unforgettable scene. The dragoon's green saddle blankets and uniforms and the plaid uniforms of the Scottish Highlanders stood out like beacons of pride.

It seemed more like a grand parade than the beginning of a battle. One thousand men advanced to attack another thousand men.

All at once, they shouted a loud, "Halloo!"

General Morgan then shouted, "They gave us the British halloo, boys. Give 'em the Indian halloo!"

Our whole army unleashed some deafening war whoops. This release of energy inspired us and made us eager to begin the fight. Colonel Washington and some of his officers told us to hold steady, which we did.

When the British front line marched within fifty yards of our sharpshooters, I heard the pop, pop, pop of rifle fire and, even from three hundred yards, I saw men falling, mostly from horses. The British line didn't falter in the least and they kept closing the gap as their drums tapped a steady beat. The sharpshooters kept shooting, but retreated, tree by tree, toward the second line of militia commanded by Colonel Pickens and his officers. More and more British officers fell, but that bright red line kept advancing.

The sharpshooters broke off their skirmish and ran back through the militia line and kneeled down to reload. When the British got within fifty yards of the militia line I saw one of our men step forward and make the first shot. It was Christopher, of course. He was the only bare-headed man in the line. Captain Tate was there too, on his horse. I could recognize his red floppy hat anywhere. And Colonel Brandon, also on his horse, stood out clearly. I sent up a quick prayer for my company and our regiment. Then the entire line opened up with sporadic firing on the enemy. British infantry fell by the score, but the rest stopped, knelt, and opened fire on our men. Some of our men fell, but not as many as on their side. Once again their muskets weren't as accurate as our rifles, but they loaded much faster and scattered more lead than we could. I could see that their bayonets were in place, ready to do their deadly deeds.

"Three shots, boys. Two more to go," the general said out loud.

I knew how much courage it took to stand in the open trying to load your rifle with an enemy firing at you. The range between the two opposing lines had narrowed to within thirty-five yards. Our men fired a second shot and the British second rank unleashed another well executed volley. I glimpsed Colonel Brandon riding up and down our infantry lines and thought I saw Colonel Hayes too, but things were getting confusing as the lines wavered, men fell, and layered smoke began to cover parts of the field.

"One more shot, boys," the general shouted.

They couldn't hear him, of course, but I guess he just wanted to cheer them on. Then their cannons fired at us. These frightening weapons caused serious damage to the center of our line. Our cannons fired back at theirs.

"Sounds like Liberty and Independence are earning their keep," Colonel Washington said.

The noise reminded me of the time my brother John made me put the wash tub over my head and he pounded on the sides with a hickory stick.

The enemy's line appeared somewhat disoriented for lack of officers, but they still came forward to within twenty yards of our line. They could start a bayonet charge at any moment. Some of the militia troops ran toward the rear now, but most stood firm and fired their third shot after which they quickly retreated toward the Continentals. The British recovered from the volley and charged, just as Morgan predicted.

I could still see most of the action because the wind blew steadily now. Our militia ran toward the flanks of our third line, the Continentals. It looked like a rout and the British fell for the ruse. I wondered when we cavalry would be allowed to swoop down on the enemy. Then I noticed Tarleton and about forty of his dragoons riding their splendid horses toward the left flank of our retreating militia.

"My God, they'll be cut to pieces," I shouted and pointed to the dragoons. The dragoons rode straight for our men in the Little River regiment. My heart raced. To my relief, General Morgan gestured to Colonel Washington to intercede and we dashed off to the rescue. We outnumbered Tarleton's dragoons, but they already slashed at our fleeing men. Blood flew and men died. In less than twenty seconds though, we smashed into them. Our attack startled them greatly and they realized they'd become the hunted rather than the hunters. I was proud of ole Dot. She performed flawlessly.

I slashed wickedly at the first green coated dragoon I came to. My blade caught him under his arm as he raised his sword too late. It was a solid connection and the man dropped his weapon and slumped over his saddle horn. I didn't wait to see where he went. I saw another dragoon coming straight at me, but before I could get in position to defend myself, Uncle Thomas raced by me. He nearly slashed the man's head clean off his body. Then he smashed into the next man's horse slashing and thrusting. Those dragoons shouldn't have attacked his defenseless infantry.

I galloped to my left around some fighting men and found another dragoon who had just delivered a head cut to one of our infantry. He didn't get to enjoy his score for long as I thrust my sword clean through his body severing his spine. He flopped off his horse moaning and spitting blood. Ole Dot let out a cry and nearly bucked me off her. Some British Dragoon had fired his pistol at me, but it hit poor

Dot in the neck. She didn't go down, but was seriously wounded. I patted her and blood covered my hand. This sent me into a rage, and I started toward the cur that shot her. Just then the British Dragoons retreated and I missed my chance to avenge Dot.

Meanwhile, the British Regulars continued their pursuit of our militia. Colonel Washington's bugler sounded assembly and we rode off to the side to regroup. Dot kept making a coughing sound. I hoped she could hold up through the battle, but she was getting weak.

From somewhere I heard the bagpipes of the Scottish Highlanders. They marched just behind the British Regulars into the thick of the fighting. Thankfully, most of our militia infantry made their way behind the Continental line to reload.

The Continentals fired on the advancing British infantry. I could tell it was the Continentals because they had the discipline to fire in unison with great precision. Then I noticed about a fourth of the Continentals on our right flank turned about face and walked to the rear. They had either been given a wrong order or they misunderstood an order. In either case, this break in the line could cost us the entire battle.

The British again thought they had a rout and ran after our retreating troops with bayonets prepared for action. Another large group of British Dragoons also saw the break in the line and swooped into the breach. Colonel Washington saw these events and led us straight toward the advancing dragoons. I saw General Morgan and his staff racing to the breach.

When the British infantry and the Highlanders got within ten paces of the Continentals, General Morgan commanded about face and gave the order to fire. They complied and fired with devastating effect. Over half of the British in that line fell dead or wounded.

Some of them simply threw down their muskets, fell to their knees, and held up their hands in surrender. This panicked the rest of their infantry and our flanking militia closed in and surrounded their main army including the reinforcing Highlanders. Dot mustered all her strength and ran fairly well, but she was fading fast.

We yelled like madmen and crashed furiously into the rear of the dragoons. Horses fell down, men screamed, and swords glinted in the sunlight and clanged together. Things seemed to move in slow motion. I saw the astonished look of one man when two of us slashed him at the same time. He dropped his saber, but kept slashing with his arm and clinched fist as he fell backward off his horse. I noticed he had a particularly fine gray gelding and almost without thinking, I jumped from my horse to his and rode after another foe. But they retreated and our bugler called for assembly again. We reformed our cavalry unit to get prepared for whatever came next. That was the last time I ever saw ole Dot. She was the best horse I ever owned.

British infantry began leaving the field and some ran back down the Green River Road from whence they came. But Tarleton's dragoons weren't finished. It was obvious they were preparing to make another charge on us and the Continentals. Colonel Washington told the bugler to sound "Charge" and off we went in a two-ranked line galloping toward the dragoons a third time. We rode right through their retreating infantry, past their two cannons, and slammed into their cavalry.

They were more prepared for us this time and gave us quite a fight. I had my hands full when a very tough Tory slashed at me from behind. Luckily, I saw it in time to deflect with my sword. His horse turned and he slashed at the back of one of my men. His saber cut down through my trooper's neck and blood spurted a yard or more up in the air. I heeled my horse and he jumped toward the Tory coward. I thrust my sword through his body just below the rib cage on his right side. He wouldn't be attacking anymore people from behind.

They held us at a stalemate until some of our militia who'd retrieved their horses joined us and fired their pistols at the enemy. I never was so glad to see Christopher as then. He rode past me and shot a dragoon off his horse. Bobo and Collins came right behind him along with Uncle Thomas and Captain Tate. I was mighty proud to see my friends join in the fight that way, especially Collins who usually did his best to avoid taking risks. The British Dragoons broke off and sped for the woods. Some went down the river road.

In a minute or two more, the British fully retreated. Old Dan Morgan's plan worked perfectly. The Partisans spontaneously gave shouts of jubilation. "Huzzah! Huzzah!" we shouted. But the battle wasn't yet won. Tarleton gathered about fifty dragoons from the woods and charged us again. We positioned ourselves around his two field artillery pieces and waited for the impact. I suppose Tarleton didn't want the dishonor of having us capture his cannon a second time.

I turned my horse just in time to avoid a side arm stroke from a green coated demon. I countered with a thrust, but missed. Then another sweeping saber caught my attention and I nearly fell off my horse ducking it. This time I reined my horse toward my opponent, deliberately running into his horse and throwing the man off balance. I thrust my sword into his shoulder and he withdrew in haste. I really liked my new horse. He had just saved my life!

As I looked for another enemy, I saw Colonel Washington leading a counter charge after the British Dragoons who were reforming about thirty yards away. One dragoon broke rank and raced straight toward our colonel. Colonel Washington struck at his opponent and his sword hit wrong and broke in half. Just as the dragoon drew up to slash our defenseless colonel, the colonel's little orderly shot the dragoon with a pistol. He fell backward to the ground.

Washington's orderly then jumped down, retrieved the fallen man's sword, and handed it to our colonel. The Colonel turned in time to parry a sword trust from Tarleton himself. We mounted militia fired our pistols from horseback and Tarleton and his men retreated at a gallop in all directions. Tarleton made a miraculous escape since I think most of us shot at him.

This all happened in less time than it takes to tell. It was almost like make-believe except the carnage and the moaning men and horses proved it to be real. The British drums had stopped. The battle lasted about an hour. Now we had really won the day, but even our army was in disarray at that moment. Some of the mounted militia from my regiment shouted, "Tarleton's Quarter," and I saw Major Jolly and six or seven others riding down the road after the fleeing British. I couldn't let them go without me so I put my heels to the flanks of my new gelding and flew after them. The chase was on!

Hit and Run by Dan Nance

CAPTURED

By riding hard, I caught up with Major Jolly and his little band and we stopped for a moment to plan our mission.

"Captain Young, nice to see you made it out with all your limbs," Jolly said.

"And my neck!" I gulped down some water from the canteen tied to my new horse's saddle horn.

After some hasty greetings, Jolly suggested we should be after their baggage wagons and we might be able to capture some good plunder, meaning food and ammunition, for the cause. I reloaded my pistol during this brief stop and gave my new horse the rest of the water in the canteen.

Since wagons moved slowly and had to stay on the road we set off after them, alert and full of anticipation. We went about twelve miles and captured two British soldiers, two Negroes, and two horses laden with leather cases of officers' clothes and pewter dinnerware. One of the cases also held paymaster gold in it.

"We'll take the Devil's money to do the Lord's work," Jolly said. "Why in thunder did Tarleton have gold with him?" I asked. "Beats me, but you'd better take it and the prisoners and return to the Cowpens post haste. We'll keep moving and see what else we can capture."

I protested, but Major Jolly insisted I should return with our prisoners and prizes, especially the gold. Jolly's party dashed off and I was left alone with the gold and the prisoners.

I walked my new gray charger at a leisurely pace and talked to my prisoners who walked ahead of me. They weren't disagreeable, but were concerned about how they would be treated by us. I assured them we Partisans and Continentals treated our prisoners better than we were received by them and their Tories. After a few miles, I noticed a party of British Dragoons coming down the road straight toward me.

With no time to lose, I wheeled my horse, heeled him hard, and started down the road in the opposite direction. My only hope was to catch up with Major Jolly and his men before they caught up with me. My horse was stiff, however, from all the exercise that morning followed by the leisurely pace we'd taken for the past half hour. The British quickly gained on me. I wheeled abruptly to the right into a small cross road, but a party of three dragoons dashed through the woods and intercepted me. I drew my pistol and aimed at the closest one and pulled the trigger, but it misfired. I threw it to the ground and drew my sword. They already held their swords high above their heads, ready for action.

I figured this was the end for me since I had to take them all at once, but I resolved to sell my life as dearly as possible. I never fought so hard, but in a few minutes a slash split one finger on my left hand wide open. Then I received a deep cut on my sword arm by a parry which disabled it. I shifted my sword to my left hand. In the next instant someone cut across my forehead with a saber and the skin slipped down over my eyes. The blood blinded me and I couldn't see anything. Then I felt the thrust of a saber through my right shoulder blade and another cut laid my left shoulder open to the bone. Lastly, I felt a powerful blow on the back of my head and I collapsed on my horse's neck, dropping my weapon.

Strong hands dragged me off the horse and I fell like a bag of grain to the ground. To my great surprise, they remarked that I was so young to be such a strong fighter and a kindly British Major ordered them to spare my life and sew up my wounds. I was mighty grateful.

All that stitching stung like hornets and made me woozy, but I was just happy to be alive. They gave me some water, stripped me of my weapons, and helped me back up on my horse. I was now a prisoner of war. I must have been in shock since my wounds didn't hurt much, except for my finger. I could feel blood seeping from my head wound down my neck, but only a little.

When we joined the larger British party at the crossroads, two Tories were with them.

"I'll be a crooked-legged dog if that ain't Thomas Young. Lookie here, Sergeant Kelly, see if it ain't so," George Littlefield exclaimed.

"It sure is him in the flesh, Captain," Kelly replied as he looked me over.

Littlefield pulled his pistol from his belt, cocked it and leveled it at my face. "Now we'll see who gets the last laugh you cocky little wart. Say your prayers, boy, afore I put you out of your misery."

I could see the seething anger in the man's eyes and I had no doubt he intended to kill me. I tried to think about what John would do in this situation, but nothing came to me. I was on my own.

"Hold up there, Captain!" the kind British Major stepped in be- tween us. "This is just a boy and he's my prisoner. And you're a damned coward for threatening him."

"He may be young, but he'll kill you fast as a rattler." Littlefield stepped toward the major. "He's nothing but a damn rebel."

"Not another word from you, man, or I'll have you in irons."

This major must have been a revered leader because over twenty soldiers drew their swords to kill Littlefield if he didn't withdraw. Fortunately, that ended the confrontation, but I kept my eye on Littlefield for as long as he was around.

A little later, the British noted my horse was a fine gelding and had a British Dragoon's saddle. They took it and put me on a small pacing pony as we rode east toward Tarleton and the main body of the British army, such as it was.

Toward evening our group caught up with Colonel Tarleton's party not far from the Broad River. They had stopped to let the horses rest. It was here that George Littlefield tried some more mischief.

"I accuse this prisoner of being one of those that robbed the women's camp while we were fightin' this morning," Littlefield said, pointing his boney finger at me.

"Search the prisoner," ordered the British major. He shot Littlefield a hard look.

They searched all of my pockets and found less than fifty cents in change.

"This change isn't worth much more than a Continental dollar," stated James Kelly as he showed it to the major.

"This boy is innocent, Littlefield, and I don't want to hear any more of your accusations," the major told him. "Mount up, we're moving out."

As I rode past Littlefield he whispered, "Your times a coming yet. I'll see you dangle from a rope afore it's all over."

Even with this threat, the thought crossed my mind that I was lucky it was Littlefield and not Bloody Bill who confronted me. Cunningham would have killed me without hesitation.

About ten minutes later, they took me to Colonel Tarleton for questioning. I did my best to keep from being cowed by this famous British officer.

They led me on my pony up to Tarleton. He was a handsome man in his late twenties and, to my surprise, had a gentlemanly manner. He wore the same uniform I'd seen him in at the Blackstock Plantation. He smiled and asked me to ride beside him so we could talk.

"What's your name, son?" "Thomas Young, sir." "How are your wounds?"

"They throb some, but they sewed me up pretty good, I reckon."

"How old are you?" "Seventeen today, sir."

"You picked a fine day to have a birthday, son." He chuckled a little and I felt comfortable with him.

"Where are you from and what unit did you fight with?"

"I'm from the Little River District of South Carolina and I'm with the Little River regiment of mounted militia."

"How many dragoons did Morgan have?"

"He had seventy dragoons and two volunteer companies of mounted militia. But you know those militiamen seldom fight," I added.

"By God, they did today!" he replied. His response greatly pleased me.

He asked me many questions and I told him the truth on all but one. He asked me whether General Morgan was reinforced before the battle. I told him he was not reinforced, but he expected to be at any moment.

I sensed Colonel Tarleton respected me and I asked him to parole me. He told me that if he did, I would go off to fight him again. I told him that was very probable, but he could exchange me for three of his men since I held some value to our regiment as a company commander. He was impressed with my rank at such a young age and agreed to request my exchange once we reached General Cornwallis's army. "In the meantime," he told me, "don't try anything smart. My men have orders to shoot any prisoner trying to escape."

I thanked Colonel Tarleton and dropped back to ride with the privates and another captive. I learned the other prisoner was Maurice De Sausseur, one of our young scouts who had been captured when Tarleton's dragoons swept down on him early this morning before the battle. We hit it off right away. He served with a North Carolina regiment from Charlotte. After exchanging information and the details of our capture, we immediately conspired to escape. We didn't know exactly how we would escape since I rode a pony and he rode a run-down nag, but we decided to stay on the lookout for any opportunity.

As we rode along, sometimes in silence, I had time to think about Father, Mother, Jane, Elizabeth, and little Andrew. I wondered if I'd ever see them again. Then I recalled Father's admonition to remember Mathew 7:7. "Ask, and it shall be given to you; seek, and you will find; knock, and it will be opened to you." I didn't know many Bible verses, but this one stuck in my head because Father favored it, I guess. As soon as I thought about that piece of scripture, my depression vanished and I became more optimistic. I also sent up a silent prayer asking God to help us escape.

I don't know if God Almighty had his hand in my circumstances at that point, but we shortly rounded a bend in the road and came upon Hamilton Ford on the Broad River. It was now fully dark, but we could see the river swelled over its banks caused by rain up in the mountains. The whole group of about eighty or one hundred men stopped to consider how to cross when a British scout came rushing up at full speed.

"Private Watson, sir," the man said to Tarleton. "Colonel Washington and his dragoons are reported to be close behind in full pursuit."

Tarleton wasted no time in telling his men to cross the river. His men objected and didn't want to cross such a roiling river, especially in the dark. Tarleton flew into a terrible rage, drew his sword and promised to cut down the first man who hesitated to cross. I'm sure the thought of losing his entire force was too much for him to bear. He cursed and swore oaths and shouted like a madman. His men evidently believed he would do as he swore to do and they rode into the water. I think I saw more of the real Tarleton at that moment than I'd experienced earlier. He was masterful at telling his subordinates how the cabbage gets chewed.

"Maurice," I whispered, "Now's our chance. Follow me into the woods."

Those British soldiers were far more concerned about crossing the river than watching out for us. And it was so dark I could hardly discern one person from another. Maurice and I slipped through the woods and went up river as quickly and quietly as possible. We moved off toward the Pacolet River and no one followed us. It was a very dark night and it rained hard. I couldn't find the ford and it was just as well, because this river raged worse than the Broad.

We continued riding up river and came upon a barn. A light shown through the siding and we heard a cough. Maurice and I dismounted and sneaked up to peek through the cracks to find that British soldiers occupied it. We then slipped back to our mounts and went on our way.

"Thank God we scouted out that barn before going in," Maurice said.

"Amen to that. And this dark, rainy night is getting more appealing by the moment. Nobody can see anything much."

Just before daylight, we arrived at Captain Hughes's place, happy to be able to stop. He ran a way station of sorts and was known to be sympathetic to the cause. I knew where his place was located, but had never stopped there before. My father once told me that Captain Hughes had fought in the French and Indian War and was well respected for his service. He and his daughter took us in, gave us some dry clothes, and fed us a fine breakfast of eggs and ham and biscuits. And she served strong tea. It was the only meal we'd eaten since dinner the night before the battle and we loved it.

Captain Hughes's daughter was a beautiful girl with red hair and a disarming smile. She charmed me beyond description and Maurice was smitten himself. Her name was Lettie.

"All right, Mr. Thomas," she said. "I see you've eaten about all you can hold, now let's look at your wounds."

"Thank you, Miss, but you don't have to do that," I told her. In truth, I'd like nothing better than to have her tend to me. Her hair flowed over her shoulders and smelled wonderful. And I liked her take-charge attitude.

"Son," Captain Hughes said, "she's as good at mending people as she is at cooking. And from the looks of you, you need some attention."

"Sit over here by the window so I can see you properly."

"Yes, Miss," I replied as I moved to the chair she was pointing at.

I could sense Maurice's envy, but he didn't let on.

She cleaned and dressed my wounds and was amazed that I'd ridden all night after receiving such cuts. They were sore as the dickens, but I sat perfectly still.

"They sliced you up pretty good, Thomas Young."

"Yes, I guess I shouldn't have been so greedy to take on three at once."

"You did no such thing!"

"Yes, ma'am, I did, but not on purpose. My horse gave out when they chased me. Then I had to fight them all."

"With all this fighting and dying, I wonder what will ever become of us. Do you think we can ever get back to normal?"

Knowing that girls always liked men who knew their verses, I said, "The good book says where the spirit of the Lord is, there is liberty. If we keep the faith, we'll win this thing." She lifted her eyebrows and nodded slightly.

"Besides, we just whipped the British and their Tory lackeys in a second major battle. They can't last forever," Maurice said.

"Those are comforting words. Now hold still. I have to get this head wound clean before it festers." She moved around behind me. "It looks like someone put a mud plaster on the back of your head." She fussed over my wounds for about a half an hour and I enjoyed her attention and the sweet smell of that rose water she wore. She finished and I felt better, but awfully sleepy.

"Now both of you go up to the loft and get some sleep. We'll take care of your horses and watch out for the enemy." I turned at the top of the stairs and saw Lettie twirling a strand of hair with one finger, smiling up at me.

"Night, Miss."

We woke up at sunrise to the aroma of eggs and sausage and biscuits. I can't remember any breakfast ever smelling so good. After living for months in the woods and eating whatever we could find, I had come to appreciate things I used to take for granted. I washed up and tried to comb my tangled hair so I might be presentable at the breakfast table. My wounds smarted something awful, but I resolved to ignore them.

"It's about time you two showed yourselves. I thought you might be sleeping all day," Lettie said.

"Sorry, Miss," we said in unison.

"Don't let her scornful ways bother you none. I'm her father and you should hear how she greets me in the morning."

"That's because you need to be prodded to get going most days. You think you're getting old, but I think you've just gotten lazy since Mamma isn't around to motivate you."

"See what I mean, boys. I rest my case."

We ate a fine breakfast and, to my embarrassment, about every time I sneaked a peek at that beautiful redheaded girl, she'd catch me and smile a little. Maurice seemed more interested in his vittles than in girl watching and that suited me just fine.

After we saddled our horses and thanked Mr. Hughes for his hospitality, we mounted up in the front yard.

"Take care that those stitches don't pull out on you and watch out for the Tories. I expect they're spread all about this country," Lettie said. Then she handed me an old loaded pistol.

"Thanks, Miss Lettie. And thanks again for your kindly treatment and for your fine cooking," I told her. I really wanted to think of something to say that would impress her, but my mind went blank and I'm sure my face turned red.

She patted my pony's neck and looked me straight in the eye. "I'd be pleased to see you again under more conducive circumstances, Thomas Young." Then, without warning, she grabbed my arm and pulled me down toward her as she stood on her tiptoes. She kissed me on the cheek, let me go, turned, and walked into the house. I was flabbergasted, but mighty pleased. It was the first time any girl ever startled me with such affection. Her kiss was warm and gentle and full of promise.

My head was still spinning when Mr. Hughes said, "Mind your back trail and don't trust anyone. God's speed to you."

We thanked Mr. Hughes and headed toward the Little River District. Maurice went on and on about my good luck with Lettie and I remarked that being on a pony was a good thing in that instance. If I'd been on that gray gelding, I would have been up too high to receive her kiss. I resolved to come back and court Lettie if the war would ever allow such a thing. I couldn't get her out of my mind and I could still smell her beautiful hair. After a while, Maurice interrupted my thoughts.

"I know you're feeling better now," Maurice said. "How's that?"

"Cause you're grinning like a butcher's dog."

"You're just jealous, but you're right. I'll probably never wash my cheek again." It excited me to think about being with Lettie in "more conducive circumstances."

LIBERTY OR DEATH

January 1781

Maurice and I rode to my home without incident and arrived by evening. Almost immediately, I came down with a terrible fever and didn't remember anything until it broke two days later. Fortunately, Uncle Thomas's wife, Aunt Elizabeth, was visiting Mother which provided two fine nurses for me. Maurice hung around until I got on the mend and gave his adieus. He wanted to get back home and visit his family.

Bobo came by for a visit and it was wonderful to see him walk into my small bedroom.

"Hey there, Captain Young. I heard you were shirking your duty and lying around in your bed over here."

"Glad to see you're in one piece, Bobo. I lost track of you during that last dragoon attack."

"Me too. It got awful confusing there at the last. I saw you riding down that road to glory, but you never came back. Got word you'd been killed."

"I thought my hide was in the loft for sure, but it'll take more than a few British Dragoons to put me under, I guess. They hacked me up pretty good and took me as their prisoner. But another captive and I put the slip on them down by the Broad River."

"I want to hear all about it. The boys back at camp will be dying for the details."

We talked for an hour or two and he told me we'd killed over one hundred and wounded another two hundred British and Tories at Cowpens. We also captured over five hundred more. "They only killed twelve of us and wounded sixty … sixty-one counting you," Bobo said.

Mother then called us to dinner. With Bobo's help, I ate at the kitchen table for the first time in days. Bobo sat across from Jane and spent most of the meal talking with her. Afterwards, the two of them went on a walk together and didn't return until nightfall. To my surprise, neither my father nor mother seemed the least bit concerned. I presumed he showed her his battle scar and all. The more I thought about it though, the more I liked the idea that my sister might have a romantic interest in my best friend.

I enjoyed having some quiet time with my father and mother. We talked a lot about the war and how we hoped the victories at King's Mountain and Cowpens might convince the British their Southern campaign was a lost cause.

"We've heard that Cornwallis is in a confused tizzy after learning about Tarleton's defeat at the Cowpens," Father said. "Some speculate that he may march back up north. Course, we'll still have to clean up the Tories if Cornwallis leaves the South. And that won't be an easy task." He rubbed his chin and added, "Galatians, chapter five says we brethren are called to liberty and we must keep fighting until we can claim it as ours. It's just as Patrick Henry said, 'Give me liberty or give me death.'"

I knew he was right and I also knew I needed to recuperate so I could get back to my company. Bobo left for camp the next day and he and Jane stood over by the well for a long time before he rode off. I felt a little better, but was still almost too weak to stand. I stayed at home for about two months to regain my strength, be sure the fever didn't return, and to get the stitches removed from my wounds. They healed up pretty well, but they left red scars and my little finger had no feeling in it.

As I slowly regained my stamina, I took Andrew squirrel hunting on several mornings. I wanted him to learn from me just as I had learned from John. He used the old small caliber flintlock I learned to shoot with and it brought back a lot of good memories. On the first morning, just before sunrise, we slipped up to the ridge where the hardwood trees grew.

"Let's sit here where we can lean back against these trees. There are several old den trees around here and you can bet that they've buried plenty of acorns and hickory nuts in the ground. There may even be a few left on the trees. So sit still, keep your eyes open for movement and listen for nutshells falling through the leaves." It was chilly, but still as could be.

"Okay," Andrew whispered.

At sunup, the finches and wrens began to sing their morning songs and a crow caw-cawed his way across the sky. Then a squirrel barked and another answered. I could hear them chasing each other around the broad trunk of an oak tree, but couldn't see them.

"What's that noise, Thomas?"

"That's two squirrels chasing each other around that big oak over yonder. Just sit still until they show themselves." Andrew tensed up and watched for movement. Then they both came into sight running down the trunk and stopping on a limb.

"Shoot the closest one."

Andrew raised the rifle slowly and took careful aim. Then a shadow crossed over head and a red-shouldered hawk swooped silently down to capture one of the squirrels. Quicker than a wink, the hawk latched onto the closest squirrel with its sharp talons and carried him off and up above the trees.

"Wow! Did you see that, Thomas?"

"That's only the second time I've seen anything like it. Looks like we're not the only hunters in these woods." The second squirrel disappeared, but it didn't matter much. Witnessing such drama in the woods excited us to no end. It's one of those things you'll never forget. Andrew jabbered about the incident for three or four minutes before I could calm him down.

"Okay. Let's just sit still now and let things quiet down. Mother is expecting some squirrel meat today."

Fifteen minutes later Andrew pulled on my shirt and pointed toward what sounded like rain drops falling through the nearby hickory leaves.

"That's a squirrel eating a hickory nut up there. Move real slowly and see if you can spot him." Andrew moved like a cat stalking his prey. After a moment, he gestured to me that he could see the squirrel.

"Okay now. He's up there real high, so get a rest for the rifle. And remember to shoot for the head." Andrew placed the barrel into the fork of a small sapling, secured his aim and fired. The rifle cracked and the squirrel fell down through the branches and plopped on the ground about ten feet away. Andrew jumped up and ran to his prize.

"It's my first squirrel," he grinned. He held it by the tail and I saw that he had made a perfect head shot.

"Not too bad for your first try. He brought the animal over and showed it to me. I slapped him on the back and he hugged me. "Sit back down and let's see if another one comes out," I said. "And reload the rifle." Andrew reloaded and sat still with his eyes focused upward.

I whispered, "John taught me that shooting squirrels and shooting men were a lot the same and he was right. You have to outsmart them. Just sit still and wait for your opportunity to see them before they see you. Of course, if you're in a big battle, things are different. You're mostly shooting into the smoke hoping you get them before they get you."

Andrew was a quick learner and the little toot shot several over the next three mornings. We dined on squirrel stew one evening and had fried squirrel the next. This made Andrew and the rest of us very proud. I told him about John's lesson on quail hunting and promised to take him next fall.

I helped my father build a false floor in the wagon so he could hide the ammunition, firearms, grain, and other provisions for our regiment as he traveled across the countryside. It was a dangerous business because one never knew when a squad of Tories would appear. If they found anything that might support the Patriot cause, they would kill Father without hesitation. Bloody Bill Cunningham might kill him just for the sport of it whether he found anything or not.

On a bright, but cold Saturday morning, I hugged my sisters and my mother and shook hands with Andrew and my father and rode off to the regimental camp. It was less than a two hour ride, but it gave me time to contemplate things. I looked a whole lot different than when I first rode off toward the camp with Uncle Thomas. I rode a pony rather than a fine horse, I carried the old pistol Lettie gave me rather than my fine rifle, and I had no knife or sword. I also carried the scars of a sword fight and the unpleasant memories of losing several friends in battles and skirmishes. I thought of my brother and how much I missed him. Like my father, I figured if General Greene could somehow defeat Cornwallis, we could do our part to rid the land of those marauding Tories and peace could return to the Carolinas.

My company and the regimental officers, including Colonel Hayes and Uncle Thomas, greeted me as I rode into our base camp. I was most pleased to see my old messmates including William Kennedy who'd recovered from his wounds received at Stallions' Plantation. He was seated at the base of his favorite old tree, smoking his pipe.

"Will you look here," James Collins called out. "Captain Thomas is back from the dead." Everyone jumped up with big grins on their faces.

"I told you he'd be back soon," Bobo said. "Nobody can keep Thomas down for long."

"Welcome back, Young, it's good to see ya," William Kennedy shot out his hand in greeting. Seeing William again warmed my spirit. He'd taught me so much during that first month of my service in the militia and he treated me like a brother.

"You're a sight for sore eyes, William, and I'm glad you're back with us," I said. "How does that wrist look?"

"It looks a darn sight better than the last time you saw it. But it looks better than it works." He held it up for me to see. It was mangled up pretty badly. "Course, I only need one hand to shoot with."

"Yeah, and he'll be a better shot with one hand working than most of us who have two," Collins said.

"Where's Christopher?" I asked.

"He helped transport the prisoners to Salisbury over in North Carolina," Bobo said. "You should have seen him out there fighting alongside his father. I expect he shot more British than anyone along the line. It pleased our colonels and they commissioned him as a lieutenant. He's second in command of the prisoner's guard. The men elected Collins to replace Christopher as sergeant.

We talked all afternoon and into the night about the battle and each other's experiences. Captain Tate, whom I owed my life to, had performed admirably and it was rumored he'd soon be promoted to a major's rank. The men elected William as a lieutenant. They all inspected my scars and listened to my stories. My sword fight and Tarleton's interrogation drew the most interest. I told them about Maurice and our escape, but I didn't tell them about Lettie Hughes for fear they'd tease me about her. Besides, I didn't want any of them to know she was so beautiful. They might get it in their heads to go over and spark her themselves.

As I left their camp for the officer's quarters, Collins followed. "I'm real glad you're back, Thomas."

"Thanks, Collins. That's a compliment I'll happily accept. And congratulations on your promotion. It is long overdue."

"You've become a good leader and fighter … a long ways from your horse killing days and we're all real proud for you, seriously proud." Collins patted my shoulder, smiled and walked back to his camp. Laws, laws, I thought. If that don't beat all.

The next morning, I retrieved my rifle from the quartermaster where I'd left it before the battle at Cowpens. I also picked up a new sword and knife. Best of all, I got a new horse, a roan-colored mare who had a deep chest and appeared to be a fine animal. At the morning officers' briefing I visited with Allen Tate and the other officers who had taught me the ways of war. We didn't have much time for a reunion because Colonel Brandon gave an extended report.

Sadly, we learned that General Morgan had petitioned to retire from service and General Greene had given his blessings. General Morgan suffered from lumbago, was old, and had already given five hard years of service in the field. Greene reunited his two Continental forces and harassed Cornwallis's army whenever he could.

Cornwallis's army was twice the size of Greene's, but Greene could out maneuver Cornwallis and strike when least expected. Our superiors ordered us to support General Greene when requested and capture the British and Loyalist garrisons throughout the backcountry. Militia General Francis Marion, the "Swamp Fox" as most folks called him, had attempted to retake Charleston at the end of January and Colonel Brandon said he would have succeeded if he'd had any artillery. But for now, our port city was still occupied by the British and their allies.

In the middle of March, General Greene, with his Continentals and Patriot militia, had fought a huge battle at Guilford Courthouse about sixty miles northwest of Charlotte. Cornwallis commanded the field after the battle, but Greene's men killed or wounded over five hundred British while losing less than half that number themselves. We were all buoyed by this news.

Thinking about Lettie Hughes also buoyed my spirits so I wrote her the news about General Greene and Guilford Courthouse and about how I had a fever for so long, but was back soldiering again. It took a lot of courage to write her, not knowing if she'd care to write back. Maybe she'd found a new interest by then and maybe that goodbye kiss was just a kind gesture. But I finally decided that if she laughed at my intentions, I would never know it and I couldn't be embarrassed like I was with Patsy Lynch. I sealed the envelope and sent it out with the next post rider.

In late April, General Greene attacked the British at Camden, or Hobkirk's Hill they called it, but was forced to retreat from the field. However, the British were so badly beaten up they abandoned their fort there. Greene's strategy was to choose where to fight, do as much damage as possible, and save the army to fight another day. In this way, he whittled away Cornwallis's army, battle by battle. This is when we were called back into action.

In a regular morning officers' meeting in early May, General Pickens, who had been promoted, addressed Uncle Thomas. "Colonel Brandon, General Marion has requested our assistance to help him secure the Tory garrison, Fort Motte, down on the Congaree River. Take two companies and render him the assistance he requests. With any luck, we can clear the backcountry of all the British."

"Yes, sir," Colonel Brandon replied. "We'll move out at noon today."

"Take plenty of salt for the men. You'll be down in that low country. It's May already and it's getting warm down there." I liked the general and admired him for being out in the field with the rest of us.

I rode over to see my old messmates, knowing they could hardly wait to get back into some action.

"Hello, Captain," Bobo greeted me as I rode into their camp. "Hey, Lieutenant Bobo. Hello, men. Got anything to eat?"

Collins said, "We've got two courses to choose from, corn dodger or dodger corn." He gave me a big grin which exposed his white teeth and accentuated his crooked nose. He reminded me of a court jester.

I dismounted and tied my horse to a tree limb just outside their camp. Two new boys were visiting their mess, Horace Spratt and Billy Reagan. They couldn't have been over fifteen and were green as grass. Christopher was talking to them as I walked over.

"It's not your mother's recipe boys, but after a while you'll learn to appreciate anything you can eat that doesn't eat you first."

"Yeah," Bobo chimed in, "and you'll soon learn to eat whenever you can. Meals don't run on regular schedules in the militia."

"And you'll notice none of us veterans have much fat on us," Collins said, pinching his trim stomach. "Anytime we find something to eat, we eat … possum, pumpkins, or persimmons; it don't matter."

"Won't be long before the wild strawberries ripen," Christopher said. "Then we'll teach you how to make our famous Little River cobbler. It'll put a grin on your face and a little meat on those skinny bones."

I sat down on a stump near the two new recruits. "While everyone's giving out advice, I'll share some, too. When the fighting starts, don't try to prove how brave you are." I glanced at Christopher. "Or take unnecessary chances." Christopher threw up his hands as if he were innocent of any such behavior. "This war isn't about individuals; it's about winning liberty for everyone. We need every man to stay alive so we can win the cause. In fact, staying alive is a real valuable skill." I pitched a stick into the cook fire.

"And we'll win. The good book says where the spirit of the Lord is, there is liberty. So stay optimistic and don't forget your nightly prayers."

It dawned on me that I sounded like my father. Just a year ago Christopher, Bobo, and I joined up and received the same advice. But it seemed much longer than a year since that transpired.

I shared their meal with them and enjoyed their bantering before fetching my horse to ride back to my camp.

"Hold up a minute, Thomas," Christopher said, as he followed me to my horse. I could tell something serious was on his mind. He lowered his voice. "I wanted to tell you how much I appreciate you and I'm glad you're my cousin."

"You're not getting soft are you?"

"No. I'm still as tough as anyone in the regiment, but you've helped me understand it's not good to be so hot-headed. I really have nothing to prove to anyone and I thank you for it." He stuck out his hand to shake mine and I hugged him instead.

"You're more like a brother than a cousin," I told him.

"Thanks. But don't expect me to be perfect. Not everyone can be as calm as you." He untied my horse's reins and handed them to me.

"See you later," I said as I mounted up and rode off. If he only knew what went on inside me before every battle or anytime I was around girls, he wouldn't think I was very calm.

We rode hard for a day and a half and arrived in time to reinforce General Marion. He was much smaller in stature than his reputation would have you believe. His troops had already surrounded the garrison and held it under siege. The British seized the area shortly after taking Charleston a year earlier, built a palisade of vertical logs around the Motte plantation house, and used it as a garrison for storing provisions and protecting their traveling armies. Marion's men dug trenches up close to the fort and waited for the British to surrender.

In a siege like this one, there's no immediate call for cavalry, so we camped out of gun range, corralled our horses, and took our turns in the trenches that more or less surrounded the fort. Just after our arrival, some of our scouts saw smoke from the fires of another British force that camped across the river within a day's travel of us. General Marion determined we could wait no longer for them to surrender. We heard him consult with the matron of the house, Mrs. Rebecca Motte.

"Mrs. Motte, we've got an enemy rescue party across the river about ten miles from here. We must either burn the British out of your home or abandon the mission."

"I'd prefer the house be burned to the ground than for it to continue protecting those red-coated devils. They've killed my Samuel and eaten all our grain and livestock." From the sound of her voice and the look on her face, nobody doubted her resolve.

"Then it'll be done post haste, Madam. Captain Smiley, fire the house."

Trouble was, no one really knew how to get close enough to set the house afire without getting shot. After learning about this dilemma, Mrs. Motte went into an outbuilding and returned with a bow and some arrows her late husband received when trading with Indians some time back. They dipped the arrows in tar pitch, lit them, and let them fly. Several of them struck in the cedar shake roof and set it on fire.

The British attempted to put out the fire on the roof, but we shot them as they tried. In short order, Lieutenant McPherson, their commander, surrendered. Things were looking up. Then to my surprise, both our men and the British set about to save the house. With great effort they put out the fire and saved Mrs. Motte's home. In gratitude, she cooked a fine dinner and served it to the commanders from both sides that evening. That was the only time I saw British and Partisan militia eat together. We rode back to the Little River District and prepared to disperse to our homes until further notice.

Just before leaving, a post rider dropped by and shouted out the names of those in our regiment who had mail. We loved to hear our names called because we seldom got letters. When we did, we read them over and over and usually shared them with our friends. My name was called and my heart rate increased as I walked over and received a letter. It had a small red heart-shaped wax seal on the envelope. I covered it with my hand and put the letter inside my shirt. It was a letter from Lettie.

"Who's the letter from, Captain Young?" asked Bobo.

"It's from Elizabeth. I didn't want him to know anything about my love interest. If he did, he and the boys would spread it all over the regiment and they would most likely pester me to death with questions.

I said my goodbyes again and mounted up. I read the letter twice as I rode home. She thanked me for writing, said she was sorry for the fever and had feared that something bad had happened since she hadn't heard from me. She went on some about her father and his lazy ways, but the last part warmed me like a fireplace in January. "… I have missed you greatly and would consider it an extraordinary kindness if you'd call on me at your earliest convenience. Perhaps we will have more conducive circumstances this time." Signed, "Affectionately, Lettie." My heart jumped up into my throat each time I read those words. I figured I'd visit my family a day or two then ride over to Mr. Hughes' place and take Lettie up on her invitation. But as luck would have it, we were pressed back into service only two days later.

On the next day, we rode southwest to take the garrison at Orangeburg. This important post provided protection for the British and their allies along the main road from Charleston to Fort Ninety Six. General Sumter commanded this engagement and it ended almost before it started. The British fired at us from a large brick house and they shouted a lot, but did very little damage. Sumter positioned an artillery piece and fired it at the end of the house. After three direct hits, the British and their Tory friends surrendered. We never even fired our rifles. It was a pleasure to behold.

We celebrated the evening with the food and drink we'd captured. Many of us decided to camp in the barn and sleep on the hay. It was much more comfortable than sleeping on pine needles. They could stick you in the worst places.

"Have another drink of this applejack, Captain," Bobo said. I'd joined my old pals at their spot in the barn. "This is the best I've tasted since we sneaked some from my father's stash down at the well house that time." We had four or five quart bottles of the liquor.

"If it's that good, pour me a full cup, Bobo." He filled a tin cup with relish. I had no way of knowing whether it tasted good or not since I'd tasted it only once before. It burned my throat all the way down just like the last time. I nursed my cup all evening, but didn't let on that I didn't favor it. In truth, I'd much rather be drinking a glass of Jane's sweet tea and singing to Major Dillard's fiddle music. But it didn't matter. What mattered was that my men were enjoying themselves. Times like these came seldom and far between.

"It's things like this you boys will remember to tell your grandchildren," William said. "We've just taken out two main garrisons and we're eating British beef and drinking British liquor." He sucked in some smoke from his pipe and blew two big, floating smoke circles.

"Yeah, but who knows what tomorrow holds," Collins offered. "We could be starvin' again like so many times before. We'd better eat everything we can while we've got it."

"There you go again, Collins. You'll never change your stinkin' thinkin' ways will you?" William asked. "Why don't you talk about that sweetheart you're so fond of or something?"

"You're not likely to hear me speak of her tonight." "Why not? Has she got you a little perturbed, maybe?"

"You could say that. Got a letter from her last week and we're goin' our separate ways I figure. Says she's tired of waiting for me."

"So that's why you've been moping around. Sorry, James. I was jilted once myself and I know how it feels," William said. "Guess she wasn't the right one for you or she would have stayed true."

"Oh, don't feel sorry for me. I'm through with women and will be better off for it." Collins stood up and grabbed a bottle of alcohol. "I think I'll nurse this here 'Scotch pint' until I pass out."

"My father says you can't live with women or without them," offered Christopher.

"There's some truth to that notion," William replied.

"But I don't think all women will let you down or pester you to death," I said, thinking about Lettie. She was on my mind just about all the time and I had written her two more letters.

"I know you're skilled in the ways of fighting, but didn't know you were that experienced in the ways of love, Captain Thomas." William observed. I was called out and had to think fast to keep Lettie a secret.

"I haven't had much experience in a romantic sense, but I know my sister Jane is every bit as smart and courageous as any man.

And I don't think she'd mistreat any man either. What do you think about that, Bobo?"

Bobo's face turned as red as a ripe tomato.

"Why are you asking Bobo about Cousin Jane?" Christopher asked. "Is he sweet on her?"

"You'll have to ask Bobo about that," I replied. "All I know is that anytime she comes around, he gets all cow-eyed and follows her all over the place."

Bobo threw a harness at me and frowned.

"Don't be striking an officer, Bobo. That's a capital offense," William said.

"I didn't strike an officer, I struck a skunk!"

"What's wrong with you anyway, Bobo?" Christopher asked. "Jane's a mighty pretty girl and she's built like a brick outhouse."

"You're right. She's a mighty pretty girl and I'm not the least ashamed of saying I'm taken with her."

"And I'm happy about the whole affair, Bobo," I said. "Perhaps you'll someday be my brother-in-law."

"Let's not get me married just yet."

"What's the matter, isn't she good enough for you?" Christopher asked. "Course, she is. I just don't know if I could stand being directly related to Thomas." That's when I threw the harness back at Bobo.

We camped there for a few days of rest, waiting for our next orders. While there, I volunteered to lead a special squad made up of about ten of our best horsemen. We planned to capture some horses the British billeted out near Bacon's Bridge in the low country. This expedition worried me because the British and Loyalists patrolled all over that unfamiliar country and we were definitely outnumbered.

We rode mostly at night and kept to the least-used roads and the woods sometimes to avoid being detected. In an all-night ride, we managed to slip past several British patrols and reached our objective. We surrounded the little stable house and corral. I led two men up to the front door and knocked. In less than a minute, a man inside asked who was there. I told him we'd come for the horses and, to our astonishment, he stuck his head out a window thinking we were his Tory friends. I grabbed the hostler's neck, drew my knife and held the sharp edge next to his Adam's apple. A tiny trickle of blood ran down his neck and into his shirt. "Open the stable door or I'll split you like a hog." I told him. The hostler did not long consider my command and opened the door with haste. We seized twelve good horses and rode back toward our Orangeburg camp. About an hour into the ride, Private Regan rode as point man down the moonlit road and motioned for us to stop. I rode up to him.

"Captain Young, there's a light up ahead."

Sure enough a light shined low, probably a lantern, and it moved straight for us. I looked back and saw another light coming up behind us.

"Off the road, men. We've got company," I said. We scattered across both sides of the road and into the woods. "Dismount and tie up the horses."

Perhaps it's some travelers just passing through," said Bobo.

"It's more likely the enemy coming after their horses," Christopher said.

"No one rides at night in this country anymore unless they're on a military mission or just plain stupid," I said. "Tie up the horses and kneel down. Get ready for action, follow my lead, and don't shoot across the road at each other."

The lights were about five hundred yards away in both directions and coming fast. Privates Reagan and Spratt tied up the horses well behind us and we knelt down behind trees. "Shoot only at my command and shoot up or down the road, not across it," I told the men. I didn't want them to shoot each other. Three minutes of silence passed and we heard the hooves of many horses coming up from the south and fewer coming down from the north. Two more minutes passed and the riders got closer and the hooves got louder.

Someone from the smaller South-bound group called for a halt, just thirty yards from our position. The North-bound group also stopped about thirty yards from us.

"Hello," someone from the smaller group shouted. "Do ye be for liberty or agin it?"

"Long live the King!" someone from the larger group replied. Then all cane broke loose. The Partisans from the small group fired their pistols and rushed for the woods. Muzzles flashed brightly and the pistols sounded more like cannons in that quiet, damp air. The Tories cursed and fired back. Their bullets whistled up the road and one horse screamed and went down spilling its rider.

"Let 'em have it," I shouted. Almost in unison, my men and I fired at the Tories. Two men in front fell and the rest scattered off in all directions. "Hold your fire; hold your fire," I shouted. "To you Whigs in the woods, we are mounted militia from the upstate Little River Regiment. Who are you?"

"We're serving under Sumter's command and hail from the New Acquisition district."

"Let's meet in the road," I said.

There were five men in their patrol unit and they were unhurt, except for that one horse. They were mighty surprised we were hiding there in the woods, but mighty grateful as well. We found the two Tories lying in the road and one was dead still; the other one was moving some.

"Bring up a lantern," I requested. Someone lit a lantern and brought it over to shine on their faces.

To my surprise, Captain George Littlefield lay on his side, dead as a stone with blood seeping from three or four bullet holes in his body. He looked smaller than I remembered and completely harmless. For some strange reason, I felt sorry for him. He'd often threatened to kill me and rode with Bloody Bill when they killed John, but I didn't hate him anymore. I realized that somewhere he had a mother and a wife and kids who would be mourning his death.

"It's Littlefield," Bobo said. He rolled the body on its back for a better look. "How about that."

"He's finally come to a sad end," I said. "Let's see the other one." "He's alive, Captain," Private Reagan said.

It was his side kick, James Kelly. "How badly are you hurt, Kelly?"

"It's you, Thomas. I might have known," he said. He coughed and spat some blood into the dusty road. "Could I have some water please? I think I'm done for good." He pointed to a bullet hole in his left lung and another in his abdomen.

Some of the men propped him up and he sipped water from a canteen. He coughed and thanked us.

"What were you doing out here at night?" I asked.

"Littlefield and I were dispatched with ten others to retrieve the horses you all stole from us. I told him not to ride with that damn light on, but he insisted on lighting it occasionally to check your tracks."

"You were right and Littlefield's ignorant ways got you both killed, it seems. I'll help you, James. You never did me a wrong. What can we do for …?" He slumped over and died before I could finish the sentence. "That's war for you, fellows," I said. Too bad the good ones have to die with the bad ones. James just got caught up with the wrong crowd."

"What shall we do with these bodies?" Private Reagan asked. Bobo said, "Let the Tories bury the Tories. That's what they do to us." "Lay them side by side next to the road so their friends can find them," I said. "And put their hats over their faces." Instead of feeling proud of our little victory, I mostly felt sorry for James Kelly.

We mounted our horses and rode unmolested back to our Orangeburg camp hoping for a good long sleep. That hay loft in the barn made for good sleeping, but I got precious little of it before someone awakened me in time for the morning officers' meeting.

"Gentlemen, General Greene and his force are this minute moving toward the settlement of Ninety Six to put the British and Tory fort under siege," Colonel Brandon said at an officers' meeting. "We'll strike the camp and be off to join him within the hour."

The fort at Ninety Six had long been a thorn in our side since it stood in the middle of our country and seemed impregnable. It was the last Tory stronghold in the backcountry and Bloody Bill Cunningham often quartered there. I prayed I could find him.

We rode out in haste and joined Greene on the twenty-fifth of May. General Greene and his troops already surrounded the large earthen fort which resembled an eight pointed star. Greene was a tall, handsome man with a stiff left leg. But this infirmity didn't affect his ability to command. He was clearly in solid control and looked like a general in his cream-colored waist coat with dark blue collars and matching breeches.

We tried many tactics to overtake the fort, but none of them worked. One unit tried to tunnel under the fort, but the enemy discovered the trick and the plan was abandoned. Another unit built a rolling tower so men on top could shoot over the enemy's wall, but the British and Tories placed sand bags on their walls to make them higher and they shot our men on the tower like fish in a barrel. One of my men was wounded in this hazardous game. It was one of the Walker brothers who lived down Bush Creek about three miles from us. They shot him as he popped his head up to take a look. Fortunately he was only grazed, but he would be out of action for a week or more.

We tried trench warfare, but our men got caught in a cross fire from the sides of two star points every time they got close. We pretty much cut off their water supply, but they sent naked Negros out before moonrise each night to get fresh water.

"We could still stop their water supply," Squire Kennedy said to me. "We'll have them plum afraid to send anyone out."

"What you got in mind?"

"Let's ease down there along the pines above the well and wait till dark. Then we can shoot the water carriers."

"But how will we see them?"

"The moon will be full up early tonight."

We both winged our first targets, but our success didn't last long. They placed sharpshooters to shoot at our gun flashes. They came very close to hitting me and one shot nicked the Squire on his left arm. Not wishing to die at this game, we gave up the effort and walked back to our campsite.

"Guess we about shelled our corn before we shucked it," Squire said.

He could fashion his words better than most anyone I knew. I guess it was because he had some college education. "We gave it a good try though," I said. In truth, I felt relieved at not having to shoot any more innocent men. How could I ever explain such a thing to Lettie? I prayed about it that night and asked God to forgive me, but I didn't know if he would. I worried myself half sick about what I'd done, but finally determined that we were just fighting the enemy the best way we knew how.

After a month of waiting and having almost one hundred men killed or wounded, General Greene broke off the siege and marched back to the High Hills of the Santee area in South Carolina. It was a shame we couldn't take the fort because I thought Bloody Bill would be there, but I, along with everyone else, agreed with the general's decision to abandon the effort.

Shortly after that, the British abandoned their fort at Ninety Six. They wanted to consolidate their forces to beat Nathaniel Greene's army. After this, the Tories in the area joined the British Regulars in the east and things returned to normal in the backcountry. We now controlled all of the backcountry Carolina outposts including the upstate area. We had accomplished our mission. We rode back to the Little River District and disbanded until we might be needed again. We officers all promised to stay in contact with each other. Allen Tate invited us all to visit his plantation on the Broad River and we promised to do so.

Disbanding my company was a hard thing, but leaving my old pals was even harder. Jim Collins' eyes welled with tears as he said goodbye. I bit my lip and awkwardly stroked my hair, but couldn't think of anything to say except the usual difficult farewells. My old messmates and I promised to stay in touch with each other as we shook hands, then rode off down the dusty roads and trails of the upcountry toward our homes. My thoughts were all jumbled up. I was sad about splitting up the regiment, eager to get home for a while, and excited about the prospect of riding over to see Lettie sometime soon.

It was early June and I'd been fighting the war for just over a year. It seemed strange to be back at our small plantation, tending the livestock and farming with my father and Hank and them. It was stranger yet to be sleeping in a bed. I still wanted to even the score with Bloody Bill, but I was satisfied I'd done my part for liberating our country. Still, my father's admonition to mind Thomas Jefferson's words rang in my head. "Eternal vigilance is the price of freedom." Besides, the war wasn't over and it was still anyone's guess who would win between General Greene and Cornwallis.

Things were peaceful in the upstate country. So peaceful, I decided to ride over to Hughes' station and visit Lettie. In her latest letter, she reminded me to come and visit. It was a full day's ride, but I made it without incident. As I rounded the bend in the road that led to their home, I took off my hat and smoothed my hair as best I could. My heart began to pound faster and I couldn't do a thing to slow it down. My mouth began to dry up and I could feel perspiration in my hands, just like that time with Patsy Lynch. But then I remembered her letters and those red wax hearts and my confidence returned. I heeled my horse and rode straight to the house.

Before I got to their short lane, Lettie burst out the front door with her beautiful red hair flowing behind her. It was a sight I've never forgotten. All my anxiety disappeared and I loved this girl for caring about me so. She threw herself into my arms and kissed me fully on the mouth. It sent shivers through my body and I knew I would never be the same.

I stayed for three days and nights and we had a wonderful time with each other. We talked for most of every day and night. She was a good horsewoman and we rode to some of her favorite spots along the river. We liked the same authors, the same songs, and she was a Presbyterian just like me. I enjoyed Mr. Hughes' stories, especially about the French and Indian War, and I liked the friendly way Lettie needled him and how he mostly ignored her jabs.

And I loved Lettie's cooking. In fact, everything about her pleased or intrigued me. As I left early that last morning, she embraced be, kissed me for a long time and gave me that little bite again.

"That's your come back kiss, Thomas. Be safe and write often."

"I'll be back as soon as the harvest is in. December, most likely. Believe me, that come back kiss has worked its magic on me." I rode home with a song in my heart and a smile on my face. I couldn't wait until December.

I didn't tell the family much about Lettie. My sisters would tease me and tell everyone at the meeting house about it. I let on that I was just really fond of Mr. Hughes, his being a hero of the French and Indian War and all. Fortunately, our district remained peaceful and we gathered in a lot of grain, but in September, General Greene's men attacked the British at a settlement called Eutaw Springs, about forty miles northeast of Orangeburg. Each side deployed about twenty-two hundred men in the fight. Greene's forces had won the day, but his men stopped to examine the British food and booty they'd captured. The British counter attacked and drove Greene's troops from the field. Both sides lost heavily. The British left the site a day or so later and marched toward Virginia, drawing an end to their southern campaign. General Greene stayed in South Carolina and pursued the remaining British and Tory troops.

On October nineteenth, Cornwallis surrendered at Yorktown, a peninsula village on the Virginia coast. General George Washington and French allies, Rochambeau and Lafayette, came down from the north and surrounded Yorktown by land. In the meantime, the French hemmed in Cornwallis from the sea by posting two fleets of ships in the harbor. Church bells across the entire country sounded off and people celebrated in the streets when Cornwallis finally surrendered. People shouted for joy anywhere they happened to be when they heard the news. That essentially ended the war for most of the country, but final liberty, we learned a month later, would still extract a terrible price in the South Carolina backcountry.

WAR MAKES BEASTS OF MEN

October 1781

Cornwallis's surrender changed everything. France and the Netherlands, followed by other European nations, formally recognized us as an independent country. Formal negotiations to separate from Great Britain were underway. The Continental Congress hurried to form a new national government and our South Carolina Provincial Assembly eventually moved to Jacksonboro and worked hard to form our new state government. They might have been beaten at Yorktown, but the British and their Tory friends still occupied our capitol city of Charleston a month later. The lobster backs still occupied New York City also, but they were expected to leave soon.

Everyone was ecstatic over our hard-fought liberation from King George and his Parliament. The Tories, however, were very angry they had lost the war and some of their units stayed active. Bloody Bill Cunningham, for example, continued to harass the countryside, mainly along the Reedy River just west of us.

I helped with the harvest at our place and, before I realized it, the month of October passed and November had begun. Our militia regiment had disbanded, but, like the Massachusetts Minute Men of 1776, we stood ready to reform at a moment's notice and stayed in close contact with each other. In fact, Colonel Hayes was entertaining many of his former militiamen and their families that same afternoon over at his tavern. My family and I would have been there, but we needed to get in the last hay cutting before it rained. We planned on going over later that evening. A little before five o' clock, we raked up the last of the hay when Hank shouted and pointed to a rising column of dark smoke off to the east.

"That's smoke from a burning building," Hank remarked. "A grass fire burns white smoke, but that's black smoke … a house most likely."

My heart leaped in my breast. "That's in the direction of Hayes Station," I said. "I've got to go, Hank. Quick, saddle our horses. I'll go get Father." I ran to the house and shouted for my father. We grabbed our rifles and bullet bags and ran to the horses. Everyone followed us out to the porch and looked at the black pillar of smoke off to the east.

"We'll be back soon, Catherine. Better get everyone into the house. Lord only knows what's going on. Hank, get the fowling piece and keep a strong lookout," Father said. "If Tories come, run out the back and hide in the woods."

Mother yelled at us as we dashed off. "You be careful, William. Mind your health. Thomas, look after your father and come back as quick as you can." She bit her lip and held Andrew to her bosom.

Mother's admonition rang in my head as we rode down the lane and turned onto the Ninety Six Road toward Hayes' Station. We intersected with several other heavily armed neighbors, including Major Jolly, as we galloped down the road. We saw the wisps of smoke from a second fire about a mile from the first. This was a classic sign of a Tory raid, but it seemed improbable since the last major battle in the backcountry was at Eutaw Springs in early September and Cornwallis had surrendered at Yorktown a month ago.

As we closed to within a mile of the fires, we still couldn't see what was burning, but it was definitely in the Hayes' Station vicinity. We heard gunshots in the distance and we spurred our horses to increase the pace. We rounded a bend and saw the cause of the first and largest fire. It was Colonel Williams' home. Someone had set it ablaze and it burned furiously. Even from that distance, we could tell the marauders were nowhere in sight.

A few minutes later Hayes' Station came into view, and it stood untouched. But the old Cherokee War blockhouse, some two hundred yards up the hill from Hayes' Tavern burned like tinder wood. We split into two small groups of about five men each and raced up the hill toward the block house.

I couldn't believe the scene we beheld. Tears flowed down my cheeks and anger rose in my breast as I surveyed that field of death. Dead bodies lay scattered throughout the small meadow surrounding the blockhouse. Our brave men who fought so hard for independence lay there hacked to pieces. Arms and legs and torsos and heads were strewn all about. Only three bodies were left undefiled. I recognized Colonel Hayes and Daniel Williams and I saw little Joseph Williams lying about twenty yards apart from the other two. The enemy had disappeared and I was never so frustrated in my life.

I wanted to kill the men who committed this terrible butchery, but there was no enemy to fight.

No one said anything at first. We were shocked numb at the horrible scene we beheld. "My God, my God," Major Jolly said over and over.

We all witnessed the death and destruction of war, but never had we seen anything like this. Over the crackling of the fire, I heard grown men sobbing as they recognized their friends. I cried along with them, half from frustration at not finding an enemy so I might avenge this atrocity and half from seeing Daniel and Joseph lying there motionless. I hadn't felt this way since learning of my brother's death.

Slowly, a few of the men who escaped this hell came out of their hiding places and told their story. The first of them was little Peter Griffin, a boy about twelve years old who had run to the block house with his father.

"They tried their best, but there were too many of them," Peter explained. "Where's my father? Has anybody seen my father?" He cried pitifully as he wandered among the decapitated bodies. Some movement near the woods caught my eye. Someone else walked toward us.

Bobo came limping out of the woods. I rushed over to greet him.

"Bobo! Thank God you're alive." I dropped my rifle and helped him over to a stump to sit on. He looked at me with a pasty white face and a blank stare. He asked for a drink of water and Major Jolly handed him a canteen. All of our men gathered around him to hear his story.

After drinking from the canteen, he began to talk.

"That damned Bloody Bill Cunningham did this." He glanced up at us and then stared at the ground. My heart pounded with this news. "I don't know how I escaped. But when I saw Cunningham intended to murder us all; I grabbed the little Griffin boy and ran into those woods with them firing several shots at us. They shot me through the fleshy part of my leg, but I kept running. I ran until I couldn't run any longer and we hid beneath an overhang back there along Mud Lick Creek."

"Start from the beginning, Bobo," suggested Major Jolly.

"We were having that little victory celebration at Colonel Hayes' Tavern. About twenty-five of us, along with the women and children, had just sat down for dinner when big John from the Williams' place rode over and told us Cunningham and about three hundred Tories torched the General's house. Colonel Hayes told all the women and children to run for the woods and hide and he ordered us to grab our weapons and make for the old block house." Bobo paused and drank some more from the canteen. "We made it to the block house a moment before they arrived and surrounded us. We fired with good effect, but there were too many of them. We held them off for a time, but they threw firebrands upon the roof and set the block house on fire. None of us were even wounded at this time, but we knew we'd all be burned alive if we stayed in there."

Little Peter Griffin wailed piteously. He'd found his father's head and sat down and held it in his hands, crying. His whimpering broke my heart. I walked over toward him, but he stood up and walked down toward the tavern where the women and children were coming out of hiding. Everyone else was listening to Bobo and I rejoined them.

"Cunningham said he wasn't interested in any more deaths and he only wanted some Whig prisoners to go with him to Charleston from where he intended to sail to the West Indies. He said he needed us for insurance to make sure he and his men made it safely to Charleston. Colonel Hayes agreed to this proposition and we all came out." Bobo blew his nose on a dirty handkerchief.

"As we stepped out, Cunningham ordered his men to tie us up with our hands behind our backs. I recollected Colonel Hayes telling us before dinner that Cunningham had tied up some Patriots over at Cloud's Creek and murdered them all not two days ago. That's when I snatched up the Griffin boy and ran as fast as I could. Some others did the same and I think several got away."

"Did you see anything else?" Major Jolly asked.

"No, sir, but I could hear the screams of our men as the damned Tories massacred them. We hid along the creek about a quarter of a mile from here."

"I saw it, Major." We all turned to see William Kennedy walking up to us.

"What happened, Kennedy?" the major asked. William walked over and sat on the ground, like he was too weak to stand and talk.

"As they tried to tie me up, I ran just like Bobo. Then I sneaked back and watched as they tied up our men. I had no rifle and couldn't do a thing to stop what happened." He looked around at the scene and took a deep breath.

"After they tied everyone up, Cunningham ordered his men to take Daniel Williams over to that fodder pole and they hanged him. No last words or prayers granted … they just hanged the boy. His face turned blue and his legs kicked … it was awful. But he never whimpered a bit. Then his little brother Joseph, only eleven years old ya know, shouted to Cunningham something about how could he tell his mother about his brother's hanging. Cunningham walked over to the boy, and said, 'You won't have to tell her anything.' And without warning he drove his sword through Joseph's little body and he died." We gasped at this outrage and men swore oaths to cut out Bloody Bill's heart among other things unfit to repeat.

Tony Zeiss

When the cries and murmurings calmed down, William continued. "Then they tried to hang Colonel Hayes from the fodder pole, but it broke. When that happened, Cunningham drove his sword through the colonel two times and he slumped over." William paused and tears welled up in his eyes.

'Hack 'em up, men,' Cunningham commanded. 'Cut them to pieces, every last one of the buggers!' Then I couldn't believe my eyes. They butchered them alive with their swords. They executed our men in just two or three minutes. No one had a chance out of it." William hanged his head and shook in his grief and shock. Big tears dripped in the dirt.

"Did they ride off then, William?" Jolly asked. William nodded.

"Which way did they go?" "East, toward Fairforest."

"Let's get after the butchers!" I said with tear-swelled eyes.

Major Jolly turned slowly to us and said that ten or twelve men had no business chasing three hundred, no matter how much need for revenge we felt.

"There will be enough widows and orphans weeping in Little River this night," my father said. "Let's try to take care of our dead." None of us liked this situation, but we knew Major Jolly and my father were right. Then we saw the women and children coming up the hill, eyes wide and sobbing.

A week later, we heard Bloody Bill Cunningham and his men escaped to Charleston and eventually to the West Indies. For weeks afterwards I slept very little from thinking about how we could avenge such a massacre. Even until this day, I still hate the Tories for what they did to my brother, to countless innocent people, and to our brave men there at Hayes' Station. But we had gained our liberty, and with it the opportunity to create a grand republic where the nation is run for the people and by the people. And no one killed his neighbor after this period.

On one clear evening just before supper, my father and I washed our hands at the well. Red sidled up to me and I scratched his ears. My father broke the silence. "There's a season for all things. And the season for hating and killing is ended."

"Not until Bloody Bill pays."

"He'll pay. God has a long memory." He put his arm around my shoulder. "I hope you can let it go. Hate is a heavy burden and it'll ruin your life if you let it. Just leave it to God to work out … that's all any of us can do now."

"It's a hard thing you ask." I stroked my hair back with my hand.

"Try to let it go and get on with life. Look forward, not backward, son. We've won our physical liberty, now let's focus on the spiritual victory that brings peace to all."

I knew he was right and after a few weeks of working hard and pondering things, I came to his way of thinking. I finally figured John and my dead comrades would want me to move on with my life and turn to more productive thoughts, thoughts about things other than war and revenge. I'd recently received a letter from Lettie and I began to think about her and that "come back" kiss. She invited me to visit her during Christmastime and, in spite of last year's vow to spend it with my family, I decided to go. A pretty girl has a powerful grip on a young man.

At the breakfast table one crisp, but sunny morning, I ran my fingers through my hair and announced, "I'm not much needed here just now. If you don't mind, I think I'll ride over to Mr. Hughes' place and pay him another visit. I really owe him my gratitude for practically saving my life."

"I think it's a perfectly wonderful idea, Thomas," my mother replied. "Jane, fetch some of that yellow ribbon from my top dresser drawer and give it to Thomas. I'll bet Mr. Hughes' daughter would fancy it for her hair and it will make a wonderful Christmas gift."

George Washington

EPILOGUE

Each of the battles and skirmishes described in this book actually happened and Thomas Young participated in them. The locations and principal officers of these battles were also authentic. With few exceptions, each character lived and participated in the scenes as described. All of the key military officers described in the book were also real people and were involved in the battles pretty much as presented. Provided for your interest are brief histories of the book's key characters:

Barrum Bobo

Barrum was a neighbor and friend to Thomas Young. He was born in 1777 and was too young to have fought in the war, but he made for a convenient character in the story. He married and built a fine brick home at the intersection of the Piedmont Stage Road and the Old Buncombe Road. It is called the Cross Keys House because the gables exhibit a cross keys insignia and still stands near Union, South Carolina. The ground on his plantation was full of red clay and Bobo established the first and largest brick factory in the upstate of South Carolina. Confederate President Jefferson Davis and several military officers rested at this house on his flight from Richmond in 1865.

Christopher Brandon

In real life, Christopher Brandon was Thomas Brandon's nephew. He applied for his pension in 1832 and Thomas Young served as a witness to his gallant service during the war. Brandon was married soon after the war, lived in the Little River District, and was 70 when he died in 1833. He and Thomas Young attended the same church throughout their lives. Christopher is buried in the Old Union Presbyterian cemetery near Monarch Mills in Union, South Carolina.

Thomas Brandon

Much beloved for his leadership, Colonel Brandon was elevated to general after the war. He was married twice and had more than ten children. After the war, General Brandon purchased Thomas Fletchall's plantation near the Fairforest Shoals settlement, exactly where he lost his only battle when Thomas Fletchall was in command of the Tories. Brandon lived there for the rest of his life and served several terms in the South Carolina Legislature. He died on February 5, 1802, at 61 and is buried in the Old Union Presbyterian Cemetery in Union, South Carolina.

Jim Collins

Nearly the same age as Thomas, Jim actually fought in most of the battles that Thomas Young fought in, but with a different regiment from York County, South Carolina commanded by Colonel John Moffett. After the war, Jim moved to Georgia and surveyed most of the northern part of the state. He and his wife, Mary, had five children. He lived in Louisiana in his later years and died on April 14, 1840, in Red River County, Texas. Jim wrote the book, *Autobiography of a Revolutionary Soldier*. The latest edition was edited by John Roberts and published by Arco Press, New York, 1979.

General Charles Cornwallis

Lord Cornwallis led a very active military and political career after the American Revolutionary War. He was a hero to the British, served as the British Envoy to Prussia, Governor General of India, where he won a major war. He was also Viceroy for Ireland and beat a French-inspired rebellion. He returned to India and died there in 1805.

Bill Cunningham

Bloody Bill escaped to Charleston after perpetrating the massacre at Hayes' Station. Legend has it that he rode his horse to death to escape capture by the Whigs for his dastardly deed at Hayes' Station. Once within the safety of Charleston which was still occupied by the British, Cunningham gave his horse a formal burial. He caught a ship to the West Indies and lived there the rest of his life.

James Dillard

Major Dillard had four wives and had 12 children. He fought at Fort Moultrie and against the Cherokees before joining Colonel Brandon's regiment. He remained in Laurens County, South Carolina, received a pension in 1833, and died on October 4, 1836.

Mary Ramage Dillard

Local legend says Mary took in Joseph Kerr for the rest of her life. Other sources say Kerr returned to North Carolina after the war and lived with his uncle. Mary and her husband James had five children together. She died in 1840 and is buried in the Duncan Creek Presbyterian Cemetery in Laurens County, South Carolina.

General Nathaniel Greene

General Greene and his close friend, General Henry Knox, were the only two generals, besides General George Washington, who served for the entire nine years of the War of the Revolution. General Greene fought (or led) fourteen battles, and his leadership in the Southern Campaign led to the American victory. He was an immense hero, probably second in status only to General Washington. North Carolina, South Carolina, and Georgia gave him land grants and money for his southern services. Many towns and counties throughout the country were named for him. His most impressive statue is located at the battlefield of the Guilford Court House in Greensboro, North Carolina. Greene settled on his Georgia estate, Mulberry Grove, just north of Savannah. He died there from sunstroke in June of 1786 at the age of 44.

Joseph Hayes

Colonel Hayes was hanged and sabered by Bloody Bill Cunningham at Hayes' Station on November 19, 1781.

Lettie Hughes

Lettie married Thomas Young in 1787 and bore two girls, Mary and Catherine. It is presumed that she died around 1793.

Benjamin Jolly

Major Jolly settled in the fork of Tinker Creek in the upstate area of South Carolina and died suddenly on his wedding day.

James Kelly

There is no apparent historical record about the Tory, James Kelly, after the war. He likely died during the war or fled to another country.

William (Squire) Kennedy

He remained in Union County South Carolina, attended the Union Presbyterian Church with many of his revolutionary war compatriots and is buried in the church's cemetery.

William Kennedy

In spite of his wounds, William lived a long life and received a pension in 1832 while living in Wayne County, Tennessee. He married Mary Ann Brandon, sister of Colonel Thomas Brandon, his commander.

Joe Kerr

Joe lived a long life in spite of his physical challenges. After the war, he first resided with an uncle in Mecklenburg County, North Carolina, and legend has it he also spent time with Major James and Mary Dillard. He received a pension in 1832 while living in White County, Tennessee. It is unclear where or when he died, but the James Williams' chapter of the Sons of the Revolution placed a ceremonial headstone for Joe near Major James Dillard's headstone in Laurens County, South Carolina.

Captain George Littlefield

There is no apparent historical record of the Tory, George Littlefield, after the war. He likely died during the war or fled to another country.

General Francis Marion

General Marion was a hero of the war, especially in the South where he is still highly revered. Many cities and counties were named in his honor as well as a national forest near Charleston, a park in Charleston, and a park in Washington, D.C. A bill was passed by Congress in 2007 to erect a monument in his honor in Washington, D.C. He married, but had no children. He died in 1795 at the age of 63 and was buried at Belle Isle Plantation in Berkeley County, South Carolina.

General Dan Morgan

General Morgan died at age 66 in 1802 and is buried in Mt. Hebron Cemetery in Winchester, Virginia, near his plantation. He amassed a large plantation of 250,000 acres and built a home he called Saratoga after his first major victory in Saratoga, New York. He was an extraordinary hero who was much celebrated for the rest of his life. Congress awarded him a medal for his 1780 victory at the Cowpens. He served in Congress and nine states named counties after him. North Carolina named a town after him and Spartanburg, South Carolina, erected a statue to him in Morgan Square where it remains today.

Adam Steedham

Steedham was hanged shortly after the battle of King's Mountain on October 7, 1780.

General Thomas Sumter

General Sumter settled on his Home House plantation near Stateburg, South Carolina. He served in the South Carolina State Legislature and later in Congress. The sports mascot for the University of South Carolina is the Gamecock, taken from the nickname of Sumter. He lived a long life and died at the age of 98 in 1832, the last surviving general of the Revolution.

Colonel Banastre Tarleton

Upon the surrender of Cornwallis's army at Yorktown, Virginia,

Tarleton was the only major British officer who was not invited to dinner with the victorious Patriots. Despite his reputation in the colonies, he was received as a hero by Great Britain upon his return and was promoted to general, was knighted, and then was elected to Parliament and served seven terms. He had no children and died in 1833 at the age of 78. His remains are buried in Leintwardine Churchyard.

Henry Allen Tate

This character was fictitious although Major Samuel Tate was a real person and a Whig who owned a plantation on Buffalo Creek near Kings Mountain. Patrick Ferguson rested his troops at this plantation before ascending to the top of Kings Mountain.

General George Washington

General Washington was elected as the President of the Constitutional Convention and later as the first President of the United States. After his exemplary service to his country, Washington returned to his Mount Vernon plantation on the Potomac River in Virginia. He farmed eight thousand acres and died in 1799. His remains are buried beside his wife, Martha, at Mount Vernon.

Lieutenant Colonel William Washington

Colonel Washington married after the war, had two children, and settled south of Charleston. He served in the South Carolina Legislature for 17 years. He was a second cousin of George Washington and hosted him at his home near Charleston, South Carolina, in 1791. He died in 1810 and is buried in a small family plot south of Charleston near the site of the Stono River battlefields.

Colonel James Williams

Colonel Williams died as the highest ranking officer of the South Carolina partisans to lose his life in battle. He is still highly regarded as a hero of the upstate area of South Carolina. A bridge in Laurens County is named for him and it spans the Little River, for which his regiment was named. A very active Sons of the Revolution Chapter in nearby Clinton, South Carolina, is named in his honor. His remains were dug up at Fondren's Plantation early in the twentieth century and reinterred in downtown Gaffney, South Carolina. A small monument marks his gravesite on Limestone Street.

Daniel Williams

Daniel was hanged by Bloody Bill Cunningham on November 19, 1781 at Hayes' Station.

Joseph Williams

Joseph was killed by Bloody Bill Cunningham with a sword thrust on November 19, 1781. (Some historic accounts purport that he was hanged, but prevailing accounts and local lore allege he was killed by the sword).

Thomas Young

Thomas Young and his family were factually represented and participated in the War of the Revolution. Thomas actually had nine brothers and sisters including John (who was killed), Jane, Elizabeth, and Christopher (Andrew). Thomas was born on January 17, 1764, in Laurens County, South Carolina, and attended the Duncan Creek Presbyterian Church, which still exists. All militia officers in South Carolina after the War of Independence were advanced by one rank as a token of appreciation for their service during the war. The government believed this was the least it could do since most of these men received no pension or pay for their service until decades later. Thomas probably received a respectable piece of land either from warrants from the state or through the auction of land formerly owned by a Tory.

Thomas married Lettie Hughes around 1787 and they had two daughters, Mary and Catherine. He remarried in 1794 to Sarah Cunningham, probably a partisan-leaning relative of Bloody Bill, and he and Sarah had nine more children, one who was named for his brother John. (No record explains what happened to Lettie, but it is probable that she died in childbirth.)

Thomas owned a plantation a few miles south of Union, South Carolina, and attended the Union Presbyterian Church for which the town was named. Thomas's pension record from the 1830s quoted Thomas as saying he waited until his war wounds prevented him from farming before he filed for a pension, because he didn't want to place an undue burden on the county. Thomas died on November 7, 1848, and is buried in the old Union Presbyterian Cemetery in Union, South Carolina near several of his revolutionary war compatriots and life-long friends.

Major Young wrote his memoirs about the war and they were published in the *Orion Magazine* in the mid-1840s. They can be located in the South Carolina Magazine of Ancestral Research, first published in 1843 by *Orion Magazine*. It is available via the Internet.

About the Author

Dr. Zeiss was president of Pueblo Community College in Colorado and Central Piedmont Community College in Charlotte, North Carolina for a combined 32 years. He has authored 20 books in historical, educational, and self-improvement genres. He was named the 2005 CEO of the Year for all 1,200 community colleges in America by the Association of Community College Trustees. He was the founding Executive Director of the Museum of the Bible in Washington, D.C. 2017-18 and an educational consultant until 2022.

About the Book

This story chronicles eighteen months in the life of sixteen-year-old Thomas Young during 1780-81. He lived and fought in the South Carolina backcountry during America's Revolutionary War. His memoirs provide the framework for this remarkable story which exemplifies sacrifice, courage, and determination in the pursuit of liberty and in the founding of a new republic.

Readers' Comments

"Zeiss weaves a riveting tale, fantastic if based on his imagination, but this novel is grounded on the facts of a teenager's life in South Carolina's Revolutionary backcountry in 1780 and 1781. Breathtaking times as his world is literally turned upside down."

— Charles Baxley, publisher, *Southern Campaigns of the American Revolution.*

"Thomas Young exhibits the individual determination and perseverance which helped form the American character. His is the spirit of Liberty."

— David Paul Reuwer, editor, *American Revolution*

www.ingramcontent.com/pod-product-compliance
Lightning Source LLC
Chambersburg PA
CBHW070059080526
44586CB00013B/1118